I0799741

ELTeach™

ENGLISH-FOR-TEACHING 3.0 HANDBOOK

DONALD FREEMAN
ANNE KATZ

NATIONAL GEOGRAPHIC LEARNING

Australia • Brazil • Canada • Mexico • Singapore • United Kingdom • United States

NATIONAL GEOGRAPHIC LEARNING

National Geographic Learning,
a Cengage Company

ELTeach: English-for-Teaching 3.0 Handbook
Donald Freeman, Anne Katz

Publisher: Sherrise Roehr
Executive Editor: Laura LeDréan
Director of Global Marketing: Ian Martin
Heads of Regional Marketing:
Charlotte Ellis (Europe, Middle East and Africa)
Irina Pereyra (Latin America)
Senior Product Marketing Manager: Caitlin Thomas
Content Project Manager: Ruth Moore
Media Researcher: Leila Hishmeh
Senior Designer: Lisa Trager
Operations Support: Avi Mednick
Manufacturing Planner: Mary Beth Hennebury
Composition: Lumina Datamatics, Inc.

ISBN: 978-0-357-63962-7

National Geographic Learning
200 Pier 4 Boulevard
Boston, MA 02210
USA

Locate your local office at **international.cengage.com/region**

Visit National Geographic Learning online at **ELTNGL.com**
Visit our corporate website at **www.cengage.com**

Printed in the United States of America
Print Number: 01 Print Year: 2020

TABLE OF CONTENTS

FROM THE AUTHORS

This *Handbook* marks the third generation of English-for-Teaching in the *ELTeach* Program. It continues the program's fundamental commitment to support teachers as they use English pedagogically to improve their classroom teaching and their students' learning. Having the materials in print form provides teachers the flexibility to work with them wherever and whenever they want or need to. The listening and video activities as well as additional practice are available online at https://learn.eltngl.com/.

The *Handbook* builds on the collaborative, practice-based foundation of the *ELTeach* Program. The content is based on the original framework for *English-for-Teaching* developed by an international consensus panel from 13 countries. The course units prepared from that framework were written by Jamie Scanlon and Cyndy Thatcher-Fettig. We are pleased that Cyndy and Jaimie worked on adapting the original version for the new print version. The *Handbook*, like every aspect of the *ELTeach* Program, would not have happened if not for the sustained, creative guidance of Laura Le Dréan, who has been the Program's Executive Editor since its inception.

The *Handbook* introduces Research Briefs that summarize the foundational research in each area of the course. To develop these briefs, Martha Epperson and Anne-Coleman Webre reviewed international research in education and English language teaching. They identified useful, relevant findings to anchor the course content. We hope that these Research Briefs, which introduce each unit, generate thinking and discussion about the language practices in the course and their effectiveness for student learning in the classroom.

But most of all this *Handbook* is a tool for you, the teacher. We hope it will help you to teach according to your goals and to support your students in achieving theirs.

Donald Freeman & Anne Katz

WHAT IS ENGLISH-FOR-TEACHING?

IT IS A SPECIALIST LANGUAGE

Every job has a specialist language. Doctors talk to their patients using medical language. Lawyers use legal language in law courts. Airline pilots use aeronautical language when they fly airplanes. So do teachers: They use specialist language when they teach.

Teacher language includes the specific words and phrases teachers use to teach their lessons. These are the words and phrases you use to present the lesson content, to manage your students, and to give feedback to your students. The language you use as a teacher is English-for-Teaching. It makes the lesson happen.

IT IS NOT THE SAME AS GENERAL ENGLISH

Often people think that if you can speak a language, you can teach it to students. They say "native speakers" can teach because they know the language. This assumes that knowing the language in general means you also know the specialist language of teaching. It assumes that if you know general English, you will know English-for-Teaching.

This idea is mistaken. Knowing a lot of general English doesn't necessarily mean you will know the specific English used for teaching. Specialized languages, such as the languages used by doctors, lawyers, airline pilots, or teachers, are not taught in general language classes.

WHY DOES ENGLISH-FOR-TEACHING MATTER?

When you—as the teacher—use English in the classroom, it makes the language real for your students. If English can be used to get things done in teaching—to organize what students do and to talk with them about their lives—it becomes a functional part of classroom life. This shows it can be used to do other things in the world. In this way, you are making the English classroom part of the world.

THINK ABOUT IT

To get a clearer idea of the difference between general English and classroom English, look at the classroom dialogue below from Unit 2, Lesson 3.

- What do you notice about what the teacher, Ms. Choi, says?
- What do you notice about what the students say?

The teacher uses classroom English to:

A. tell students what to do.

B. tell students to speak up so the class can hear.

C. give students positive feedback.
tell students the class is over.
dismiss the class for lunch.

Ms. Choi:	*All right, everyone go to your seats, please*
Sangwoo:	*What do I do? What should I do?*
Ms. Choi:	*Sangwoo, please go to your seat. Mirae and Sangwoo, please stand up. Read the conversation for the class.*
Mirae:	*Do you like to play tennis?*
Ms. Choi:	*Please speak louder, Mirae.*
Mirae:	*Do you like to play tennis?*
Sangwoo:	*Yes, I do. How about you?*
Mirae:	*No, I don't.*
Ms. Choi:	*Very good. Please sit down. OK, good job, everyone. Now, please get ready for lunch. Line up and please be quiet.*

The students use general English to:

1. ask and answer questions from the textbook.
2. talk about what they like to do outside of class.

Now, think about your classroom.

a. How do you use English in your classroom? What do you say to students in your class?

b. How do students use English in your classroom? What do they practice saying?

Compare the two. What do you notice?

The English you use to teach	The English students are learning and using
This is CLASSROOM ENGLISH	**This is GENERAL ENGLISH**

THE ENGLISH-FOR-TEACHING FRAMEWORK

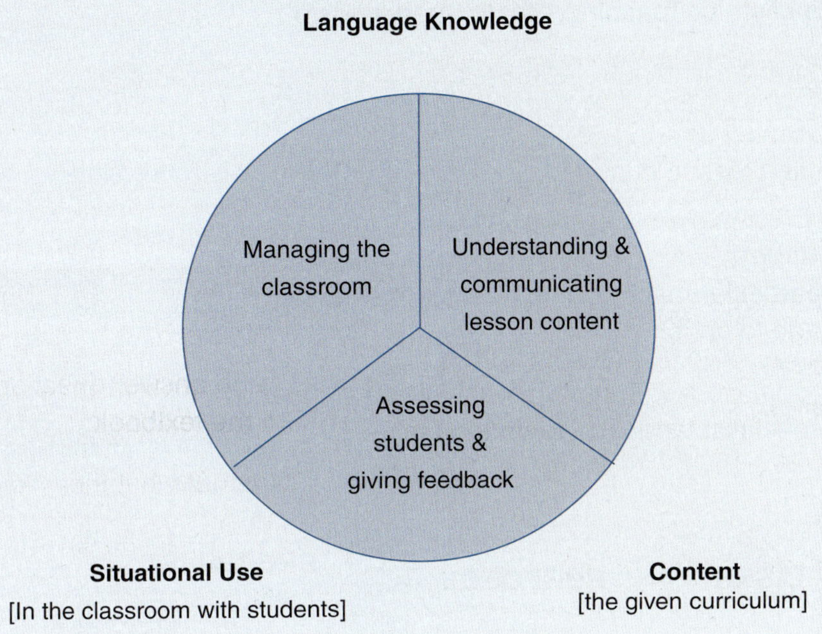

Fig 1 The English-for-Teaching Framework

Figure 1 shows the framework of English-for-Teaching, which is how the classroom language in the course is organized.

The three areas in bold around the circle create the context for the language that teachers use in the classroom.

- **Language knowledge** is the teacher's knowledge of English.
- **Content** in lessons comes from the curriculum, textbooks, and materials used in school.
- **Situational use** refers to how the teacher interacts with their students

The three sections inside the circle describe how the teacher uses language in the classroom:

- **Managing the classroom:** to organize what is happening in the lesson, give directions, provide instructions for activities, start and finish the lesson.
- **Understanding and communicating lesson content:** to be familiar with the textbook and classroom materials and to make sure students know what they are supposed to learn.
- **Assessing students & giving feedback:** to monitor students as they are working in the lesson and to give them feedback.

HOW IS ENGLISH-FOR-TEACHING ORGANIZED?

This course presents the English you use to do the classroom tasks every day with your students. You use this language—English-for-Teaching—to do three kinds of classroom work:

- Managing the classroom
- Understanding and communicating lesson content
- Assessing students and giving feedback.

Each of these can be broken down into particular tasks you do as a teacher. Each task has a purpose and specialist language to do it.

This table shows each category of classroom work with typical teacher tasks and their purposes. It also gives examples of the specialist language to do the task.

CATEGORY	TEACHER TASKS	PURPOSE	SPECIALIST LANGUAGE
Managing the classroom	Organizing students	Giving directions to students to settle down and begin work	*Please go to your seat.* *Work with a partner.*
Understanding and communicating lesson content	Setting up an activity	Giving instructions and explanations for doing an activity	*Match the questions and answers.* *Take turns to read the paragraph.* *Underline the words you don't know.*
Assessing students and giving feedback	Responding to what students say during an oral activity	Correcting students' use of the target language	*That's right.* *Nice work.* *Look at the example in the chart again.* *Those are great ideas.*

LANGUAGE RESOURCES IN THE CLASSROOM

There are three types of language in the 'language' classroom:

- Content language is what you are teaching and what students are learning. It comes from the curriculum, the textbook, and other classroom materials. It is also called the target language.
- Student language is the language(s) students use in the lesson. It often combines the target language and their home/first language.
- Teacher language is the language(s) you use when you teach the lesson. It is usually the target language, but it may also be another language that you share with the students.

It can be challenging to decide how to manage these various types of language in your classroom. The following sections explore how to manage these various types of language in the classroom.

USING ENGLISH IN THE CLASSROOM: MAKING RULES OR MAKING DECISIONS?

We want students to use the target language for what they are doing in the lesson as much as they can. The more you and your students use the target language in the classroom, the more functional and real it becomes. This is why teachers look for interesting content and motivating activities for their lessons. When students use English to talk with friends or to ask you questions, as well as to do classroom activities, the target language becomes more than content language. It becomes part of how the classroom works. This can make the target language seem less 'foreign'.

Getting students to use English, the target language, as much as possible in class can be hard to do. Teachers often think that the best way is to require students to use only English and to prevent them from using their home language. This makes it a rule.

There is an old saying that 'You can lead a horse to water, but you can't make them drink.' It usually doesn't work to require students to use English. Instead, students need to decide to use English in class. This can happen throughout the lesson, especially when students do activities that give them the chance to make choices about what to say. These many small decisions add up to their using English. These add up to their using English.

The same is true for you as the teacher. Teachers are expected to use the target language, English, when they teach. This idea comes from the established practices in the field. It is also common sense. In the Audio-lingual Method of the 1960s and 1970s, teachers were taught to make their students use only the target language in class. The goal was to build in students 'correct language habits'. The idea was also part of Communicative Language Teaching, although the goal was to make the target language as real as possible. Common sense supports this goal. It says to students that if English is a language like your first language, you should be able to make it work to do the things you want to do.

These ideas are based on structural ideas of language. Today we recognize that language use is fluid and depends on the social context.

HOW LANGUAGES ARE USED

In school, languages are generally defined as systems—of grammar, vocabulary, spelling, etc. We see this view in the curriculum and in textbooks. It is useful for identifying learning aims of language lessons. Language is also social and interactive. In today's plurilingual world, people often know more than one language, and they use different parts of these languages as they need them.

Languages are resources. People naturally use the resources they can to reach their goals. Each situation defines which resources work best. For example, in a Japanese restaurant, you might ask for 'sushi'. You probably wouldn't say 'fish on rice'. When we see languages as resources students use rather than systems they have to learn, it allows us to be more flexible in deciding which language to use in teaching.

Teachers and students have many language resources they can use in the language classroom. These resources include parts of the target language, students' first language, and any other common language they share. Mixing words and phrases from these different language systems as classroom resources may seem confusing, but it can also be effective. This process is called 'translanguaging' — 'trans' means working 'across languages'.

SOME STRATEGIES FOR TRANSLANGUAGING

There are many 'translanguaging' strategies you can use to support your students as they learn English. Some of these strategies are familiar; you may already use them in your classroom.

- Giving directions: Give the directions in English. Then ask a student volunteer to tell you what you said using the shared language of the classroom.
- Checking in: When you give instructions for an activity, check students understand by asking, "Do you understand?" or "What did I ask you to do?" Let students respond in any language and repeat what they tell you in English.
- Staying in English: When students speak to you in another language during the lesson, respond to them naturally but in English. In this way, you are each using languages as resources. You are also modeling English.
- Conversation activities: In open-ended activities like conversations or role plays, let students use your shared language for words, phrases, or ideas they can't say in English. As they are speaking, say the English version in a regular tone. The point is not to interrupt, but to give them the phrase in English.
- Vocabulary you don't know: When students ask about a word or phrase that you don't know in English, you can tell them, "Let's look it up in the dictionary." Have someone look up the word or phrase in an English monolingual dictionary and someone else in a bilingual dictionary. Compare what they find.
- 'Sotto voce': When giving instructions, making short announcements, or even calling on students, say the information first in English and then, immediately afterwards, in a quieter tone, in the shared language of the classroom. This quieter tone is called 'sotto voce', which means 'under the voice' in Italian.

UNIT 1 RESEARCH BRIEF
MANAGING THE CLASSROOM: The Learning Environment

The language and routines in Unit 1 help you manage your classroom to create a positive learning environment. Here is some research supporting this unit.

What is the classroom 'learning environment'?

The classroom learning environment has three major parts: the physical classroom, the relationship between the teacher and the students, and the classroom systems or routines that help learning. In a positive learning environment, students feel safe, relaxed, and motivated. They are willing to take risks using the new language. In a negative learning environment, students do not feel safe. They are less likely to participate and more likely to disrupt the class. Teachers recognize that creating a positive learning environment is important to student learning.

Why does the learning environment matter?

Research shows that the learning environment influences student achievement. In positive learning environments, classes run smoothly and efficiently. Teachers and students have more time to focus on learning content. In a positive learning environment, students are more likely to be interested in the content. They are motivated, and they participate more.

Research has shown that teachers' actions strongly predict successful student learning. Teachers who create positive learning environments generally do two things. First, they build interpersonal relationships with their students. Students who believe their teacher cares about them are more likely to engage in learning. Second, these teachers create classroom routines and explain them to students. Knowing classroom routines can make students feel safe and increase their participation. More involvement by students through a positive learning environment can increase their learning.

A research study

HOW DO EXPERT TEACHERS MANAGE THE CLASSROOM?

Leinhardt, Weidman, and Hammond (1987) focused specifically on how expert teachers used classroom routines to maximize[1] student learning. They chose teachers whose students consistently performed well and asked: *What routines did these teachers use? How did their routines help the class flow smoothly?* The researchers collected data such as videos, observation logs, interviews, and student perceptions[2] over two years. In the end, they identified three types of routines that created an environment that helps student learning. They called these management routines, support routines, and exchange routines. There were two key findings: Expert teachers used a larger number of these routines than beginning teachers. Expert teachers explicitly taught these routines at the beginning of the year. Over time, these routines became part of the classroom as a learning environment that allowed the teachers and students to focus on learning.

[1] maximize: to make the most of
[2] perception: opinion, thought

Research questions and findings

Below are some questions researchers have asked about how to create a positive learning environment. Findings of these studies are listed after each question.

1. **How do teachers build relationships with students?**
   Teachers . . .

   a. greet students at the beginning of class (Cook et al., 2018; Curby, Rimm-Kaufman, & Abry, 2013).

   b. learn students' names and use them (Cook et al., 2018).

   c. take time to learn about the students' backgrounds and interests and ask about their lives outside of school (teachers also share their own interests and backgrounds with their students) (Anderman, Andrzejewski, & Allen, 2011; Cheng & Dörnyei, 2007; Curby et al., 2013).

2. **What types of classroom routines do expert teachers use?**
   These teachers . . .

   a. use management routines to start and end the class (Collier-Meek, Johnson, Sanetti, & Minami, 2019; Curby et al., 2013).

   b. use routines such as how to collect and distribute classroom materials and homework (Leinhardt et al., 1987).

3. **How does a positive classroom environment impact student learning?**
   A positive classroom learning environment . . .

   a. is more predictable, which encourages students to participate (Hiver & Al-Hoorie, 2007) and can make them more likely to participate (Collier-Meek et al., 2019; Frisby & Martin, 2010).

   b. focuses more on content and less on activity transitions (Leinhardt et al., 1987; Marzano & Pickering, 2003) and can lead to better student learning outcomes (Curby et al., 2013; Frisby & Martin, 2010).

   c. can help students be more willing to communicate in the L2/English (Joe, Hiver, & Al-Hoorie, 2017; Khajavy, Ghonosolly, Fatemi, & Choi, 2016).

UNIT 1 MANAGING THE CLASSROOM: ENVIRONMENT

LESSON 1 GREETING STUDENTS

PREVIEW

You can greet your students in English. This helps them get ready to listen and speak in English.

In Lesson 1, you will:

- greet students.
- ask students about their weekend or vacation.
- reply to student greetings.

Language to Know

afternoon	break	morning	summer	vacation	weekend

What Do You Know?

Write the words or phrases you know for greeting students in English. One example is below:

Hello

Rate your confidence using these phrases. Put a check below your confidence level.

not confident	a little confident	somewhat confident	very confident

LEARN 1

A. Here are some phrases for greeting students. Listen and repeat. 1.1

Greeting Students

Hi, everyone.

Hello, everyone.

Good morning, everyone.

Good afternoon, class.

How are you?

How are you doing?

How is everyone today?

Good to see you.

How was your vacation?

Responses

Great, thanks.

Fine, thanks.

Fine, thank you. And you?

B. There are many substitutions for these phrases. Listen and repeat. 1.2

Phrases	Substitutions
Good morning, everyone.	Good morning, students/children.
Good afternoon, class.	Good afternoon, boys and girls.
How was your vacation?	How was your break/weekend/summer?

LEARN 2

Read the conversation, and watch the video. Listen to the teacher greet the students. ▶ 1.1

Ms. Silva: Good morning, everyone.
Class: Good morning, Ms. Silva.
Ms. Silva: How is everyone today?
Class: Fine, thank you.
Ana: How are you, Ms. Silva?
Ms. Silva: Great, thanks. How was your weekend, Ana?
Ana: It was good.
Ms. Silva: And how about you, Pedro?
Pedro: Fine, thanks. How was yours?

PRACTICE 1

Choose the correct answer.

1. **Good morning, ______________ .**
   a. fine
   b. you
   c. class
   d. today

2. **How ______________ your vacation?**
   a. were
   b. have
   c. was
   d. are

3. **Good to ______________ you.**
   a. say
   b. thank
   c. take
   d. see

4. **How are you ______________ ?**
   a. being
   b. doing
   c. saying
   d. going

5. **______________ was your summer?**
   a. Who
   b. Which
   c. Why
   d. How

6. **How is ______________ ?**
   a. every today
   b. everyone today
   c. every day
   d. you today

7. **Hello, Ana. How ______________ ?**
   a. are you
   b. was yours
   c. is it
   d. is it doing

8. **Fine, thank you. ______________ ?**
   a. OK
   b. Are you
   c. And you
   d. And everyone

9. **______________ doing?**
   a. How was your
   b. How are you
   c. Where is it
   d. How is it

10. **Hello, class. ______________ ?**
   a. How was your break
   b. And you
   c. Everyone
   d. And yours

PRACTICE 2

Fill in the blanks with the phrases. Some phrases can go in more than one blank.

Fine, thanks.	Hi, Pedro.
Fine, thank you. And you?	How are you doing, Ana?
Good afternoon, class.	How is everyone today?
Good to see you.	How was your weekend?
Great, thanks.	How was your vacation?

1. **Teacher:** ______________________
   Students: Good afternoon.

2. **Student:** Hi, Ms. Silva.
   Teacher: ______________________

3. **Teacher:** ______________________
   Student: Good to see you, too.

4. **Teacher:** ______________________
   Student: I'm fine, thank you. And you?

5. **Teacher:** ______________________
   Students: We're fine, thanks.

6. **Student:** How was your summer, Ms. Silva?
   Teacher: ______________________

7. **Teacher:** ______________________
   Student: It was great! I visited New York City.

8. **Student:** Hello, Ms. Silva. How was your weekend?
   Teacher: ______________________

9. **Student:** How are you, Ms. Silva?
   Teacher: ______________________
   Student: I'm fine, thanks.

10. **Teacher:** ______________________
    Student: Great! My team won the soccer game on Saturday.

REFLECT

Think about what you learned in this lesson. Write five phrases you practiced.

Phrases for Greeting Students

Now rate your confidence using these phrases. Put a check below your confidence level.

not confident	a little confident	somewhat confident	very confident

LESSON 2 DISCUSSING THE DATE AND WEATHER

PREVIEW

You can begin your lessons with a simple routine in English. For example, you can talk about the date and the weather.

In Lesson 2, you will:

- talk about the weather.
- name the days of the week.
- say the date.
- write the date and weather.

Language to Know

days of the week	months	ordinal numbers	seasons	weather

What Do You Know?

Write the phrases you know for discussing the date and the weather in English. Two examples are below:

Discussing the Date	Discussing the Weather
Today is February 2.	It's hot.

Rate your confidence using these phrases. Put a check below your confidence level.

not confident	a little confident	somewhat confident	very confident

LEARN 1

A. Here are some phrases for asking about the date and the weather. Listen and repeat. 1.3

Asking about the Date

What day is today?

What day is tomorrow?

What day was yesterday?

What's the month?

What's the date?

Responses

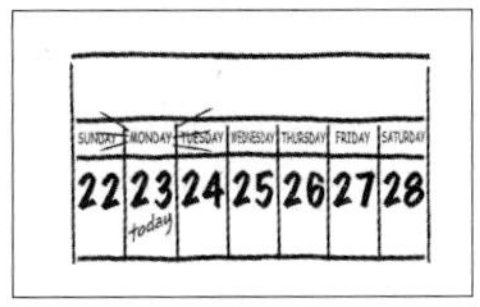

Today is Monday.

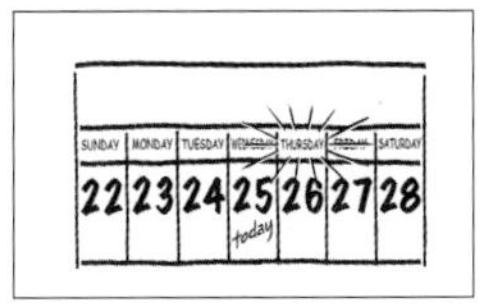

Tomorrow is Thursday.

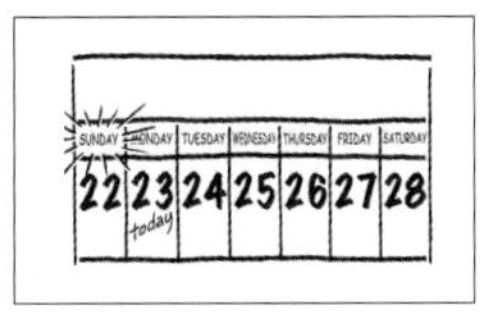

Yesterday was Sunday.

It's January.

It's April 1.

Asking about the Weather	Responses
 *What season is it?*	 *It's winter.*
 *What's the weather like?*	 *It's hot.*
 *How's the weather?*	 *It's hot.*

B. There are many substitutions for these phrases. Listen and repeat. 1.4

Phrases	Substitutions	
What's the date?	What's today's date?	
It's April 1.	It's May 2. It's June 3.	
It's winter.	It's spring. It's summer.	It's fall. It's autumn.
It's hot.	It's cold. It's raining.	It's sunny. It's warm.

LEARN 2

Read the conversation, and watch the video. Listen to the teacher discuss the date and the weather. ▶ 1.2

Ms. Silva: OK, everyone. Please look at the board. What day is today? Please raise your hands. Yes, Ana?

Ana: Today's Monday.

Ms. Silva: Very good. Today is Monday. Thank you, Ana. And what's the date today? Pedro?

Pedro: It's April 2.

Ms. Silva: Today is Monday, April 2. Great. How's the weather today? Ana?

Ana: It's raining.

Ms. Silva: That's right. It's raining today.

PRACTICE 1

Choose the correct answer.

1. **What day is today?**
   a. Today is Monday.
   b. It's March.
   c. Tomorrow is Tuesday.
   d. It's summer.

2. **What season is it?**
   a. It's today.
   b. It's sunny.
   c. It's September.
   d. It's spring.

3. **What's the weather like?**
   a. It's winter.
   b. It's sunny.
   c. It's June 1.
   d. It's summer.

4. **What's today's date?**
   a. It's October 10.
   b. Today is Monday.
   c. It's October.
   d. Yesterday was Friday.

5. **How's the weather?**
   a. It's March.
   b. It's spring.
   c. It's raining.
   d. It's Monday.

6. **What day is tomorrow?**
   a. Yesterday was Tuesday.
   b. Today is Thursday.
   c. Tomorrow is Saturday.
   d. Today is September 9.

7. **What day was yesterday?**
   a. Yesterday was Sunday.
   b. Tomorrow is Tuesday.
   c. Today is Monday.
   d. It's Sunday.

8. **Today is Wednesday. What day is tomorrow?**
   a. Tomorrow is Monday.
   b. It's Wednesday.
   c. Tomorrow is Thursday.
   d. It's February.

9. **Yesterday was Saturday. What day is today?**
   a. It's February 10.
   b. It's Thursday.
   c. Tomorrow is Friday.
   d. Today is Sunday.

10. **Tomorrow is Thursday. What day is today?**
    a. It's Wednesday.
    b. It's Friday.
    c. Tomorrow is Sunday.
    d. Yesterday was Tuesday.

PRACTICE 2

Read the situation. Choose the correct answer.

1. **Tell students what day it is.**
   a. Today is Monday.
   b. Tomorrow is Wednesday.
   c. It's November 20.

2. **Students just came in from outside. You ask:**
   a. What season is it?
   b. What's the month?
   c. How's the weather?

3. **A student wants to know the date. He asks:**
   a. What's today's date?
   b. What day is today?
   c. What day is tomorrow?

4. **A student asks, "What day is today?" You reply:**
   a. Today is Wednesday.
   b. Tomorrow is Friday.
   c. Yesterday was Sunday.

5. **A student asks, "What's the date?" You reply:**
   a. Tomorrow is Friday.
   b. It's autumn.
   c. Today is September 1.

6. **A student wants to know the day. He asks:**
   a. What day is today?
   b. What's the month?
   c. What's the date?

7. **A student wants to know if it's fall or winter. He asks:**
   a. What's the month?
   b. What season is it?
   c. What's the weather like?

8. **You are practicing the days of the week. You say, "Today is Monday. Tomorrow is Tuesday." Next, you ask:**
   a. What day was yesterday?
   b. How's the weather?
   c. What's the month?

9. **A student has just answered, "Tuesday." What did you ask her?**
   a. How's the weather?
   b. What's today's date?
   c. What day is tomorrow?

10. **A student has just said, "It's snowing." What did you ask him?**
    a. What season is it?
    b. What's the weather like?
    c. What day was yesterday?

REFLECT

Think about what you learned in this lesson. Write five phrases you practiced.

Phrases for Discussing the Date and Weather

Now rate your confidence using these phrases. Put a check below your confidence level.

not confident	a little confident	somewhat confident	very confident

LESSON 3 TAKING ATTENDANCE

PREVIEW

You can take attendance in English.

In Lesson 3, you will:

- take attendance.
- call on students.
- ask about specific students.

Language to Know

absent	ill	present	sick
call your name	late	raise your hand	take attendance

What Do You Know?

Write the phrases you know for taking attendance in English. One example is below:

I'm going to take attendance now.

Rate your confidence using these phrases. Put a check below your confidence level.

not confident	a little confident	somewhat confident	very confident

LEARN 1

A. Here are some phrases for taking attendance. Listen and repeat. 1.5

Taking Attendance

Where is Ana?

Is everyone here?

Is Pedro here today?

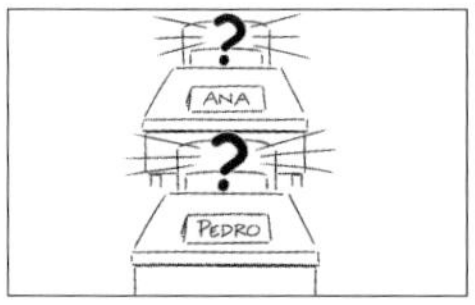

Are Pedro and Ana here today?

Who's absent today?

Who's not here today?

I'm going to take attendance now.

Please say "here" when I call your name.

Raise your hand when I call your name.

B. Here is one substitution for this phrase. Listen and repeat. 1.6

Phrase	Substitution
Please say "here" when I call your name.	Please say "present" when I call your name.

LEARN 2

Read the conversation, and watch the video. Listen to the teacher take attendance. ▶ 1.3

Ms. Silva: Good morning, everyone.
Class: Good morning, Ms. Silva.
Ms. Silva: Please listen. I'm going to take attendance now. Please say "here" when I call your name. Pedro?
Pedro: Here!
Ms. Silva: Ana? Is Ana here today?
Ana: Yes. Present!
Ms. Silva: OK. Paula? Where is Paula?
Ana: Paula is sick today.
Ms. Silva: I see. Paula is absent. Thank you.

PRACTICE 1

Choose the correct answer.

1. **______________ Ana here today?**
   a. Is
   b. Does
   c. Goes
   d. Sees

2. **______________ is Pedro?**
   a. What
   b. Why
   c. When
   d. Where

3. **Is everyone ______________?**
   a. here
   b. today
   c. there
   d. name

4. **Who's ______________ today?**
   a. attendance
   b. everyone
   c. name
   d. absent

5. **Who's ______________ here today?**
   a. everyone
   b. absent
   c. not
   d. no

6. **I'm going to ______________ attendance now.**
   a. make
   b. take
   c. raise
   d. say

7. **______________ Pedro and Ana here today?**
   a. See
   b. Do
   c. Is
   d. Are

8. **Please say "here" when I ______________ your name.**
   a. play
   b. hear
   c. call
   d. take

9. **Please ______________ your hand when I call your name.**
   a. give
   b. say
   c. raise
   d. call

10. **Please say "______________" when I call your name.**
   a. name
   b. absent
   c. present
   d. please

PRACTICE 2

Fill in the blanks with the phrases.

absent	everyone	ill	raise	thanks
call	here	late	take attendance	today

Ms. Silva: Good afternoon, class.
Class: Good afternoon, Ms. Silva.

Ms. Silva: How is ________________ today?
Class: Fine, thank you. How are you?

Ms. Silva: Great, ________________. OK, I'm going to ________________ now.
Please ________________ your hand when I ________________ your name. Ana?
Ana: Here.

Ms. Silva: Good morning Ana. Pedro? Is Pedro here ________________ ?
Ana: Pedro is ________________. He went to the restroom.

Ms. Silva: OK, who's ________________?
Ana: Paula is not ________________. She's ________________.

REFLECT

Think about what you learned in this lesson. Write five phrases you practiced.

Phrases for Taking Attendance

Now rate your confidence using these phrases. Put a check below your confidence level.

not confident	a little confident	somewhat confident	very confident

LESSON 4 REVIEWING AND COLLECTING STUDENT WORK

PREVIEW

You can check and collect student work in English.

In Lesson 4, you will:

- ask students about their work.
- ask students for their work.
- tell students what to do with their work.
- respond to students' questions about their work.

Language to Know

exchange	homework	quiz	workbook
hand in	paper	test	worksheet

What Do You Know?

Write the phrases you know for reviewing and collecting student work in English. Two examples are below:

Reviewing Student Work	Collecting Student Work
Let's check your homework.	*Please take out your papers.*

Rate your confidence using these phrases. Put a check below your confidence level.

not confident	a little confident	somewhat confident	very confident

LEARN 1

A. Here are some phrases for reviewing student work. Listen and repeat. 1.7

Reviewing Student Work

Let's check your homework.

Let's go over your homework together.

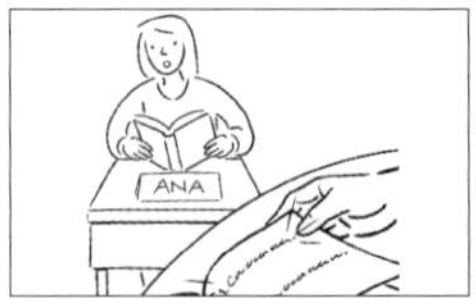

Ana, please read the first sentence.

Pedro, please write number 1 on the board.

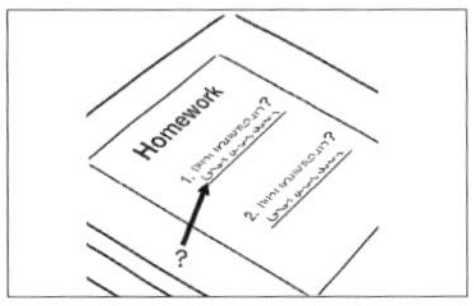
What's your answer to question 1?

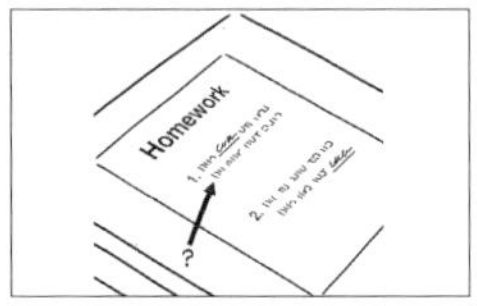
What did you write in the blank for sentence 1?

Please exchange papers with a partner.

Yes, that's correct.

No, it's not correct. Check again.

B. Here are some phrases for collecting student work. Listen and repeat. 1.8

Collecting Student Work

Please take out your homework.

Please hand in your papers.

Please put your homework on my desk.

Please bring your homework next time.

Please pass your papers to me.

Does everyone have their homework?

Pedro will collect your homework.

C. There are many substitutions for reviewing student work. Listen and repeat. 1.9

Phrases	Substitutions
Let's check your homework.	Let's check your quizzes.
Let's go over your homework together.	Let's go over your quizzes together.
Ana, please read the first sentence.	Ana, please read number 2.

D. There are also many substitutions for collecting student work. Listen and repeat. 1.10

Phrases	Substitutions
Please put your homework on my desk.	Please hand in your quizzes/homework/ worksheets. Please put your tests/quizzes on my desk.
Please bring your homework next time.	Please bring your homework next class/week.
Please pass your papers to me.	Please pass your tests/quizzes/homework/ worksheets to me.
Does everyone have their homework?	Does everyone have their workbook/worksheet?
Pedro will collect your homework.	Pedro will collect your tests/quizzes.

LEARN 2

Read the conversation, and watch the video. Listen to the teacher review the homework. ▶ 1.4

Ms. Silva: Good afternoon, class.
Class: Good afternoon.
Ms. Silva: Please take out your papers. Let's go over your homework. Does everyone have their worksheet? Yes, Pedro?
Pedro: Sorry, I forgot my homework.
Ms. Silva: OK. Please bring your homework next time. Ana, please read the first sentence.
Ana: I have a cat.
Ms. Silva: Yes, that's correct. Ana, please write number 1 on the board.

PRACTICE 1

Fill in the blanks with the phrases.

blank	have	No	on	partner
hand	me	number	out	please

1. ______________, it's not correct. Check again.
2. Ana, ______________ read number 2.
3. Please ______________ in your papers.
4. Does everyone ______________ their worksheet?
5. Please pass your tests to ______________.
6. Please put your worksheets ______________ my desk.
7. Please take ______________ your worksheets.
8. Ana, please write ______________ 3 on the board.
9. What did you write in the ______________ for sentence 3?
10. Please exchange papers with a ______________.

PRACTICE 2

Read the student's line. Choose the correct teacher's response.

1. **Student:** Is this answer correct?
   Teacher: ______________________
   a. Yes, that's correct.
   b. Let's check your quizzes.
   c. Take out your workbooks.
   d. Please pass your worksheet to me.

2. **Student:** Is this sentence OK?
   Teacher: ______________________
   a. Let's go over your homework.
   b. No, it's not correct.
   c. Ana, please read number 5 on the board.
   d. What did you write for sentence 2?

3. **Student:** What do I do?
   Teacher: ______________________
   a. Yes, that's correct.
   b. No, it's not correct. Check again.
   c. Please pass your worksheet to me.
   d. Does everyone have their workbook?

4. **Student:** Can I work with Ana?
   Teacher: ______________________
   a. Pedro will collect our homework.
   b. Yes. Please exchange papers with Ana.
   c. Please bring your homework next week.
   d. What is your answer to number 6?

5. **Student:** Sorry. I didn't do my homework.
   Teacher: ____________________
   a. Please put your homework on my desk.
   b. Yes, that's correct.
   c. Please bring your homework tomorrow.
   d. Please write number 1 on the board.

6. **Student:** Where do I put my homework?
   Teacher: ____________________
   a. Please pass your papers to me.
   b. No, it's not correct. Check again.
   c. Please put your homework on my desk.
   d. Please exchange papers with a partner.

7. **Student:** Do I hand in the worksheet?
   Teacher: ____________________
   a. Pedro, please read the first sentence.
   b. Ana will collect your tests.
   c. Yes. Please pass your worksheets to me.
   d. What did you write for sentence 2?

8. **Student:** I forgot my homework.
   Teacher: ____________________
   a. Please pass your homework to me.
   b. Let's check your homework together.
   c. Please exchange papers with a partner.
   d. Please bring your homework next time.

9. **Student:** Where do we put our homework?
   Teacher: ____________________
   a. Please hand in your quizzes.
   b. Pedro will collect your homework.
   c. What's your answer to question 5?
   d. Let's go over your homework together.

10. **Student:** Do I hand in the test?
    Teacher: ____________________
    a. Please put your test on my desk.
    b. Please take out your worksheet.
    c. Does everyone have their workbook?
    d. What did you write in the blank for sentence 2?

REFLECT

Think about what you learned in this lesson. Write five phrases you practiced.

Phrases for Reviewing and Collecting Student Work

Now rate your confidence using these phrases. Put a check below your confidence level.

not confident	a little confident	somewhat confident	very confident

LESSON 5 REVIEW A

1 Fill in the blanks with the words and phrases. Then practice the teacher's lines.

go over	Good morning	Is everyone here	next time	weekend

Ms. Silva: ________________________, boys and girls. How is everyone today?
Students: Fine, thank you. How are you?

Ms. Silva: Great, thanks. Did you have a good ________________________?
Students: Yes, we did.

Ms. Silva: Good. ________________________ today?
Ana: No. Pedro is sick today.

Ms. Silva: OK. Thank you. Let's ________________________ your homework together.
Ana: Sorry. I forgot my homework.

Ms. Silva: Please bring your homework ________________________.
Ana: Yes, teacher.

2 Write sentences for greeting the class and taking attendance. Use the key words. Then practice saying the phrases aloud.

Greet the class and take attendance.

1. morning/class ____
   everyone/here ____
2. how/everyone ____
   who/absent ____
3. morning/children ____
   take/attendance ____
4. afternoon/boys/girls ____
   raise hand/call/name ____
5. how/weekend ____
   "here"/call/name ____

3 Read and listen to the model sentences. Practice saying the sentences aloud. 1.11

1. Hi, everyone. How are you doing? Good to see you.
2. Today is Monday, October 10. What's the weather like?
3. I'm going to take attendance now. Who's not here today?
4. Let's check your homework. Please exchange papers with a partner.
5. Does everyone have their worksheet? Please pass your papers to me.

4 Look at the pictures. Describe the date and weather.

1. Today is Monday, May 10. It is ______________.

2. Today is Friday, ______________. It is raining.

3. Today is ______________. It is snowing.

4. Today is Wednesday, ______________. ______________.

5. Today is ______________. ______________.

5 **Write sentences to respond to students. Use the key words. Then practice saying the phrases aloud.**

1. What do I do?
   read/first/sentence ______________________________

2. What's today's date?
   Wednesday/May 20 ______________________________

3. Where do I put my homework?
   put/my desk ______________________________

4. I forgot my homework.
   bring/next class ______________________________

5. Good afternoon, teacher. How are you?
   afternoon/Ana ______________________________

   fine/thank you/you ______________________________

LESSON 6 MAKING ANNOUNCEMENTS A

PREVIEW

You can announce tests, quizzes, projects, and special assignments in English.

In Lesson 6, you will:
- get students' attention.
- announce tests and quizzes.
- announce projects and special assignments.
- write announcements.
- respond to students' questions.

Language to Know

announcement	chapter	group	quiz	unit
assignment	due	pair	report	

What Do You Know?

Do you know these phrases for making announcements? Write *K* if you know the phrase. Write *DK* if you do not know the phrase.

_______________ I have something to tell you.

_______________ I have an announcement to make.

_______________ Please listen carefully.

_______________ We will have a test tomorrow.

_______________ There will be a test on June 7.

_______________ The test is on Unit 6.

_______________ Don't forget to study for the test.

_______________ Don't forget about the test on Tuesday.

_______________ We are going to do a project on family.

_______________ You should finish the report by June 1.

LEARN 1

A. Here are some phrases for getting students' attention. Listen and repeat. 1.12

Getting Students' Attention

I have something to tell you.

I have an announcement to make.

I have some important information for you.

Please listen carefully.

Please write it down.

Please copy from the board.

B. There are many substitutions for getting students' attention. Listen and repeat. 1.13

Phrases	Substitutions
I have an announcement to make.	I have some announcements to make.
Please write it down.	Please write them down.
There will be a test on June 7.	There will be a quiz on June 7. There will be a test on Monday.

C. Here are some phrases for announcing tests and quizzes. Listen and repeat. 1.14

Announcing Tests and Quizzes

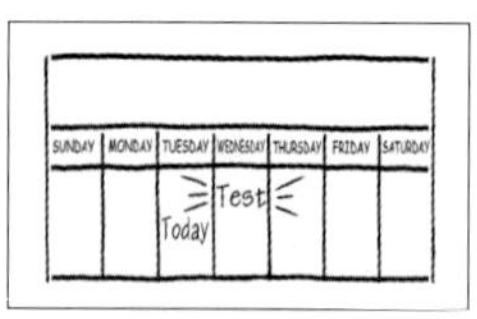

We will have a test tomorrow.

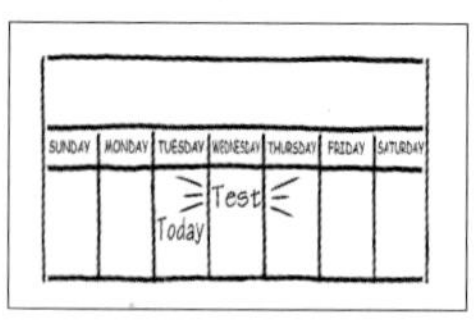

Remember that we have a test tomorrow.

There will be a test on June 7.

The test is on Unit 6.

Don't forget to study for the test.

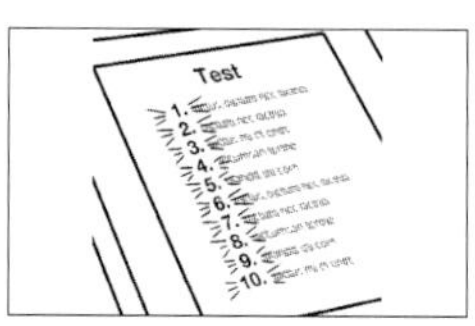

The test has 10 questions.

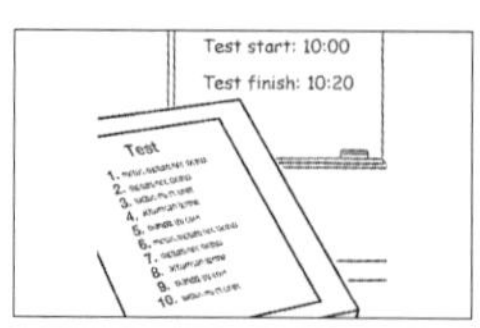

The test will take 20 minutes.

Don't forget about the test on Tuesday.

D. There are many substitutions for announcing tests and quizzes. Listen and repeat. 1.15

Phrases	Substitutions
The test is on Unit 6.	The test is on Tuesday. The test is on past tense verbs.
Remember to study Chapter 7 for the test.	Remember to study colors for the test. Remember to review past tense verbs for the test.
The test will take 20 minutes.	The test will take until the end of class.

LEARN 2

Read the conversation, and watch the video. Listen to the teacher get her students' attention and announce a quiz. 1.5

Ms. Silva: Please listen carefully. I have an announcement to make. We will have a quiz tomorrow.

Pedro: Can you repeat that, please?

Ms. Silva: We will have a quiz tomorrow. The quiz is on family vocabulary. Don't forget to study Chapter 7.

Pedro: When is the quiz?

Ms. Silva: Does everyone have a pencil and a notebook?

Students: Yes.

Ms. Silva: Please copy from the board. There will be a quiz tomorrow, May 16. Review family vocabulary. Remember to study Chapter 7.

Pedro: The quiz is on family vocabulary, right?

Ms. Silva: That's right.

LEARN 3

Here are some phrases for announcing projects and special assignments. Listen and repeat. 1.16

Announcing Projects and Special Assignments

We are going to do a project on family.

You will do a project on clothing.

The project is due on May 30.

You should finish the report by June 1.

Work on your own.

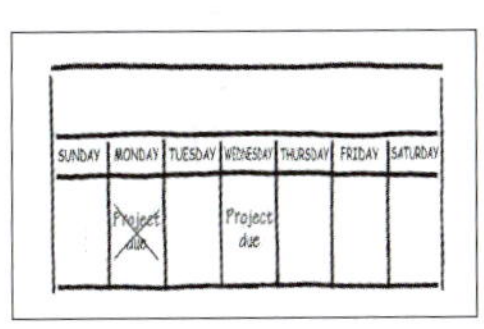

There's a new due date for the project.

LEARN 4

Look at the board. Then read the conversation and listen to the teacher announce a project. 1.17

Ms. Silva: OK, class. I have some important information for you. Please look at the board. You will do a project on your family next week. Yes, Pedro?
Pedro: What's the project?
Ms. Silva: You will make a poster of your family. Yes, Ana.
Ana: When is it due?
Ms. Silva: You have to finish the project by Monday, May 29.
Pedro: Can you repeat that, please?
Ms. Silva: The project is due on Monday, May 29.

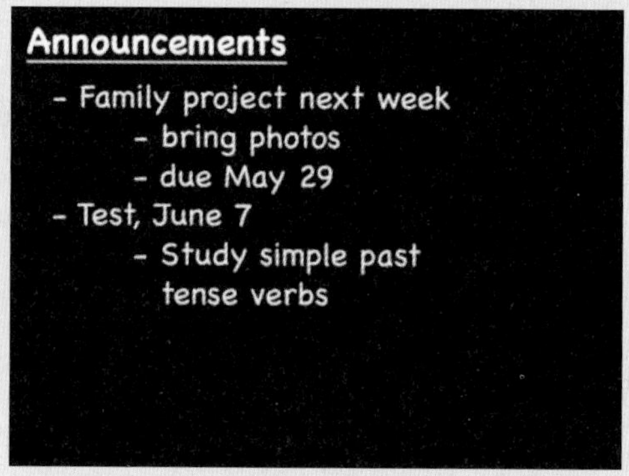

PRACTICE 1

Fill in the blanks with the phrases.

a report on your family	information for you	to do a project on food	write it down
be a quiz tomorrow	is due June 2nd	we have a quiz next week	
for the test	the quiz on Tuesday	will have a test tomorrow	

1. I have some important ______________________.
2. Please ______________________.
3. We ______________________.
4. Remember to study ______________________.
5. Don't forget about ______________________.
6. Remember that ______________________.
7. There will ______________________.
8. We are going ______________________.
9. The project ______________________.
10. You will do ______________________.

PRACTICE 2

Read the situation. Choose the correct answer. Then practice saying the answer aloud.

1. **You want students' attention. You say:**
   a. Please listen carefully.
   b. Work on your own.
   c. Please copy from the board.

2. **You are beginning an announcement. You say:**
   a. The test has 10 questions.
   b. I have some important information for you.
   c. Work in groups.

3. **You want students to remember your announcement. You say:**
   a. Please write it down.
   b. The test is on Tuesday.
   c. There is a new due date for the project.

4. **Tell students when the quiz is.**
   a. The quiz will take until the end of class.
   b. The quiz has 10 questions.
   c. There will be a quiz on Friday.

5. **Remind students about a test.**
   a. Please copy from the board.
   b. You will work on your own.
   c. Remember that we have a test on Monday.

6. **Announce an upcoming project.**
   a. You should finish the project by December 15.
   b. You will do a project on food vocabulary.
   c. I have something to tell you.

7. **You want students to write about their families. You say:**
   a. Please write it down.
   b. We are going to do a report about food.
   c. You will do a report on your family.

8. **Tell students when their report is due.**
   a. You have to finish your report by June 10.
   b. You will do a report on clothing.
   c. There is a new due date for your report.

9. **You want students' work at the end of next week. You say:**
   a. There will be a test on Thursday.
   b. Your project is due next Friday.
   c. You should finish your report by Tuesday.

10. **You are assigning work for the weekend. You say:**
   a. There will be a test on Friday.
   b. Remember that we have a quiz tomorrow.
   c. Don't forget to study for the quiz on Monday.

PRACTICE 3

Fill in the blanks with the words and phrases. Some phrases can go in more than one place.

announcements	due	new	remember	should
Don't forget	Monday	next week	report	study

Today is ______________, May 30. I have some ______________. Please listen carefully. Your project is ______________ tomorrow. Also, there is a ______________ due date for the ______________. You ______________ finish the report by June 6. And, ______________ that we have a test ______________. ______________ to ______________ Unit 3.

REFLECT

Think about what you learned in this lesson. Write five phrases you practiced.

Phrases for Making Announcements

Now rate your confidence using these phrases. Put a check below your confidence level.

not confident	a little confident	somewhat confident	very confident

LESSON 7 MAKING ANNOUNCEMENTS B

PREVIEW

You can announce schedule changes and events in English.

In Lesson 7, you will:

- announce schedule changes.
- tell students about special events.
- talk about school activities.
- write announcements for students.
- respond to student questions on announcements.

Language to Know

break	guest	invitation	notice	trip
concert	holiday	meeting	recess	visitor

What Do You Know?

Do you know these phrases for helping students self-correct? Write *K* if you know the phrase. Write *DK* if you do not know the phrase.

__________ There's a change in the schedule.

__________ We are going to finish class early tomorrow.

__________ We will have a visitor today.

__________ Tomorrow there's no class because it's a holiday.

__________ There will be a parent meeting on Monday.

__________ Don't forget about the concert tonight.

__________ Give this notice to your parents.

__________ We are coming back at 2:00 PM.

LEARN 1

A. Here are some phrases for announcing schedule changes and events. Listen and repeat. 1.18

Announcing Schedule Changes and Events

There's a change in the schedule.

We are going to finish class early tomorrow.

We will have a visitor today.

A visitor is coming tomorrow.

There will not be recess today.

We will not have a break today.

Recess will be shorter today.

We are going to read first today.

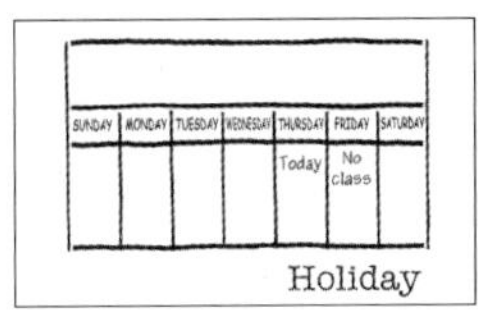

Tomorrow there's no class because it's a holiday.

B. There are many substitutions for these phrases. Listen and repeat. 1.19

Phrases	Substitutions
We are going to finish class early tomorrow.	We are going to finish class at 10:00 AM today.
We will have a visitor today.	We will have lunch early today.
A visitor is coming tomorrow.	A visitor is coming on Tuesday.
Recess will be shorter today.	The break will be shorter today.
We are going to read first today.	We will read first today. We are going to write first today.
Tomorrow there's no class because it's a holiday.	Tomorrow there's no test because it's a holiday. Tomorrow there will be no recess because we have a class trip.

LEARN 2

Read the conversation, and watch the video. Listen to the teacher announce schedule changes. ▶ 1.6

Ms. Silva: Everyone please listen carefully. I have some announcements to make. We will not have a break today. Is that clear?

Class: Yes.

Ms. Silva: Please use the time to study for the quiz. Yes, Ana. Do you have a question?

Ana: When is the quiz?

Ms. Silva: On Wednesday.

Ana: OK. Thank you.

Ms. Silva: On Thursday, there is a change in the schedule. We are going to finish class early.

Pedro: Can you repeat that, please?

Ms. Silva: Yes. We will finish early on Thursday. Also, on Friday, there's no class because it's a holiday.

LEARN 3

A. Here are some phrases for announcing school activities. Listen and repeat. 1.20

Announcing Activities

There will be a parent meeting on Monday, January 6.

We're going to have a visitor on Tuesday.

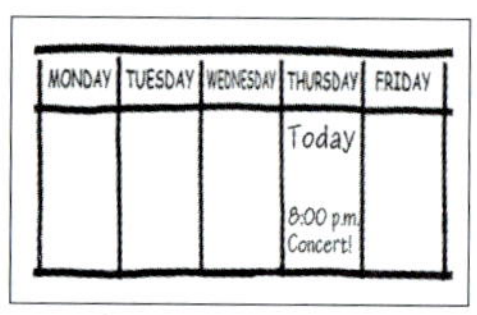

Don't forget about the concert tonight.

Tell your parents about the parent meeting tomorrow.

Give this notice to your parents.

On September 15, we will go to the zoo.

We are coming back at 2:00 PM.

B. There are many substitutions for these phrases. Listen and repeat. 1.21

Phrases	Substitutions
There will be a parent meeting on Monday, January 6.	There will be a class trip on Monday, January 6. There will be a concert next week.
We're going to have a visitor on Tuesday.	We're going to have a guest tomorrow. We're going to have a visitor on February 10.
Don't forget about the concert tonight.	Don't forget about the class trip tonight. Don't forget about the parent meeting next week. Don't forget about the concert tomorrow night.
Give this notice to your parents.	Give this invitation to your parents.
On September 15, we will go to the zoo.	Next week, we will go to the zoo. Tomorrow, we will see a play. On September 15, we will visit a museum.
We are coming back at 2:00 PM.	We are coming back at 11:00 AM.

LEARN 4

Read the class schedule. Listen to the teacher respond to student questions on announcements.

Ms. Silva: Please listen. I have some important information for you. There will be a class trip next week. Yes, Pedro?

Pedro: What day?

Ms. Silva: Tuesday, October 18. Please write it down. We will visit the museum. Ana?

Ana: When are we coming back?

Ms. Silva: At 2:00 PM. Also, we are going to have a visitor on Wednesday.

Pedro: Who's the visitor?

Ms. Silva: It's Mr. Costa from the library. Finally, don't forget about the parent meetings next week. Give this notice to your parents.

MONDAY, OCTOBER 17	
TUESDAY, OCTOBER 18	Class trip – museum, 10:00 AM-2:00 PM
WEDNESDAY, OCTOBER 19	Visitor – Mr. Costa
THURSDAY, OCTOBER 20	
FRIDAY, OCTOBER 21	Parent meetings

PRACTICE 1

Read the class events notice. Fill in the blanks with the phrases.

Class Events in October

- **Friday, October 10** - Parent meetings
- **Tuesday, October 14** - Guest: Mrs. Santos, City Garden Project
- **Monday, October 20** - Class trip (play)
- **Friday, October 24** - Concert

a guest	give this notice	parent meetings	some announcements	tell your parents

Teacher: I have ________________ to make. Please look at this notice. First, please ________________ about the ________________ this Friday, October 10.

Student: What time?

Teacher: The meetings start at 4:00 PM. Please ________________ to your parents. Then, next Tuesday we are going to have ________________ .

class trip	is coming	on October 20	the concert	write it down

Student: Who's the visitor?

Teacher: Mrs. Santos ________________ to talk about the City Garden Project. Also, remember that there will be a ________________ to see a play.

Student: When are we going?

Teacher: The class trip is ________________. Please ________________. Finally, don't forget about ________________ on Friday, October 24.

PRACTICE 2

Read the conversation. Choose the correct teacher's response.

1. **Teacher:** There will be a class trip next week.
   Student: Where are we going?
   Teacher: ________________
   a. We are going to finish class early tomorrow.
   b. There will be a parent meeting on Tuesday, September 16.
   c. We are going to visit the zoo.

2. **Teacher:** Don't forget about the concert next Friday.
   Student: Can you repeat that?
   Teacher: ________________
   a. Yes. There will be a concert next Friday.
   b. Yes. Don't forget about the parent meetings next Friday.
   c. Yes. Don't forget about the concert tomorrow night.

3. **Teacher:** Tomorrow there's no class.
   Student: Why?
   Teacher: ________________
   a. Because we will have lunch early today.
   b. Because it's a holiday.
   c. Because we are going to finish class early tomorrow.

4. **Teacher:** We are going to finish class early today.
   Student: What time?
   Teacher: ________________
   a. We will finish at 1:00 PM.
   b. We are coming back at 2:00 PM.
   c. A visitor is coming today.

5. **Teacher:** We are going to have a visitor next week.
   Student: Who is the visitor?
   Teacher: ________________
   a. Next week we will visit the library.
   b. Give this invitation to your parents.
   c. Mr. Costa is coming to talk about new books.

6. **Teacher:** We will visit the museum today.
   Student: When are we coming back?
   Teacher: ________________
   a. We will come back at 2:00 PM.
   b. There's a change in the schedule.
   c. We are going to finish class at 10:30 AM today.

7. **Teacher:** The break will be shorter today.
   Student: Why?
   Teacher: ______________________
   a. We will not have a break today.
   b. Give this notice to your parents.
   c. We are going to have a guest.

8. **Teacher:** There will be no break tomorrow. There will be a class trip at 10:00 AM.
   Student: For how long?
   Teacher: ______________________
   a. We are coming back at 2:00 PM.
   b. We will see a play.
   c. There's a change in the schedule.

9. **Teacher:** Don't forget about the class trip next Friday.
   Student: Where are we going?
   Teacher: ______________________
   a. Give this invitation to your parents.
   b. We will go to the theater to see a play.
   c. We are going to have a visitor next Friday.

10. **Teacher:** We are going to read first today.
    Student: Why?
    Teacher: ______________________
    a. We are going to finish class early today.
    b. Tell your parents about the parent meeting tomorrow.
    c. Tomorrow there's no recess.

REFLECT

Think about what you learned in this lesson. Write five phrases you practiced.

Phrases for Making Announcements

Now rate your confidence using these phrases. Put a check below your confidence level.

not confident	a little confident	somewhat confident	very confident

LESSON 8 ASSIGNING HOMEWORK

PREVIEW

You can assign and explain homework in English. This will help students learn to listen for information in English.

In Lesson 8, you will:

- announce assignments and due dates.
- write assignments on the board.
- explain where to find assignments.
- respond to student questions about homework.

Language to Know

article	assignment	conversation	interview	paragraph
assign	complete	dialog	letter	review

What Do You Know?

Do you know these phrases for assigning homework? Write *K* if you know the phrase. Write *DK* if you do not know the phrase.

_______________ Your assignment is on page 16.

_______________ Your homework is due next class.

_______________ Review the vocabulary for a quiz.

_______________ Practice the conversation on page 19.

_______________ Write sentences using the vocabulary.

_______________ For our next class, please listen to the dialog on page 20.

_______________ Your homework is to read the text, then answer the questions.

_______________ Next time, don't forget to bring your homework.

LEARN 1

A. Here are some phrases for assigning homework. Listen and repeat. 1.22

Assigning Homework

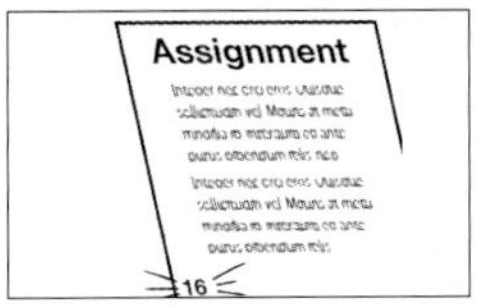

Your assignment is on page 16.

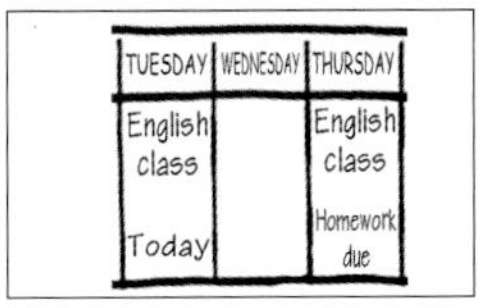

Your homework is due next class.

Review the vocabulary for a quiz.

Practice the conversation on page 19.

Write five sentences using the vocabulary.

For homework, complete the exercise on page 7 in the workbook.

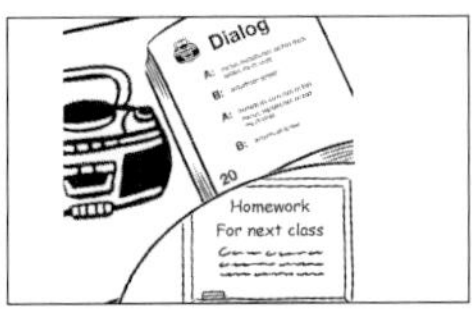

For our next class, please listen to the dialog on page 20.

Your homework is to read the text, then answer the questions.

Next time, don't forget to bring your homework.

B. There are many substitutions for these phrases. Listen and repeat. 1.23

Phrases	Substitutions
Your homework is due next class.	Your assignment is due Monday.
Review the vocabulary for a quiz.	Study the verbs for a quiz. Review the vocabulary on page 33.
Practice the conversation on page 19.	Practice the dialog in the book.
Write five sentences using the vocabulary.	Write a paragraph using the vocabulary. Write five sentences using the verbs in Unit 4.
For homework, complete the exercise on page 7 in the workbook.	For homework, complete the activity on page 7 in the book.
For our next class, please listen to the dialog on page 20.	For our next class, please listen to the interview on page 20. For our next class, please listen to the conversation on page 20.

(*continue*)

Phrases	Substitutions
Your homework is to read the text, then answer the questions.	Your homework is to read the article, then answer the questions. Your homework is to read the letter, then do the exercise.
Next time, don't forget to bring your homework.	Next time, don't forget to bring your book.

LEARN 2

Read the conversation, and watch the video. Listen to the teacher assign homework. ▶ 1.7

Ms. Silva: Please look at the board. This is your homework. Write it down. Complete the grammar worksheet. You need to do pages 1 and 2. Is that clear?

Class: Yes.

Ms. Silva: Your reading assignment is on page 72. Read the article and answer the questions. Yes, Pedro, do you have a question?

Pedro: Which book?

Ms. Silva: In your textbook. Answer the questions in your notebook. OK?

Pedro: OK. For when?

Ms. Silva: For next class. And for Friday, please do Exercises 7 and 8 on page 79.

PRACTICE 1

Choose the correct answer.

1. **Your homework is ______________ complete the exercise on page 17.**
   a. of
   b. to
   c. in
   d. on

2. **Your assignment is ______________ page 12.**
   a. in
   b. over
   c. of
   d. on

3. **Your homework is ______________ on Monday.**
   a. finish
   b. due
   c. complete
   d. read

4. **______________ our next class, please read the story on page 10.**
   a. To
   b. On
   c. From
   d. For

5. For homework, please _______________ Exercises A and C.

a. complete
b. listen
c. be
d. forget

6. Your homework is to copy the vocabulary and do the _______________ on pages 3 and 4.

a. classes
b. exercises
c. answers
d. papers

7. Next time, don't forget to bring your _______________.

a. page
b. class
c. book
d. blanks

8. _______________ your assignment for next time.

a. Bring
b. Fill
c. Listen
d. Forget

9. For homework, _______________ reading the conversation on page 15.

a. answer
b. practice
c. forget
d. do

10. For our next class, listen to the lesson, then _______________ the exercise.

a. answer
b. listen
c. forget
d. do

PRACTICE 2

Fill in the blanks with the phrases.

complete Exercise A	five sentences using	in the workbook	practice reading	Unit 2

Ana: What's the homework?
Ms. Silva: Your assignment is to ______________________ the dialog on page 10.

Ana: Which book?
Ms. Silva: Page 10 ______________________. Listen to the dialog and ______________________.

Pedro: What do we have to write?
Ms. Silva: Write ______________________ the vocabulary in ______________________.

and study for	assignment	please review the	the quiz	your homework is due

Pedro: Is the homework for tomorrow?
Ms. Silva: Yes, ______________________ tomorrow. Also, ______________________ words on page 7 for ______________________ on Friday.
Ana: Can you repeat that?

Ms. Silva: Your ______________________ is due tomorrow, ______________________ the quiz on Friday.
Ana: OK. Thank you.

PRACTICE 3

Read the situation. Choose the correct answer. Then practice saying the answer aloud.

1. **Tell students when to hand in their homework.**
   a. Your assignment is on page 26.
   b. Study the vocabulary for a quiz.
   c. Your homework is due on Monday.

2. **Tell students where to find their homework.**
   a. Your assignment is on page 5.
   b. Read the article and answer the questions.
   c. Next time, don't forget to bring your book.

3. **Tell students what to do for homework.**
   a. Listen to the conversation and answer the questions.
   b. Don't forget your homework.
   c. Your homework is due on Wednesday.

4. **You are giving a vocabulary quiz tomorrow. You say:**
   a. Practice reading the dialog in the book.
   b. Write a paragraph using the vocabulary.
   c. Review the vocabulary on page 7 for a quiz.

5. **A student asks, "What's the homework?" You reply:**
   a. For our next class, please read the article on page 10.
   b. Your assignment is due next class.
   c. Next time, don't forget to bring your homework.

6. **A student asks, "What do we have to do?" You reply:**
   a. Your homework is due next class.
   b. Complete the activity on page 9.
   c. Your assignment is due tomorrow.

7. **You want students to practice new vocabulary. You say:**
   a. Write 10 sentences using the vocabulary.
   b. Next time, don't forget to bring your book.
   c. Listen to the interview, then answer the questions.

8. **Assign a reading activity to students.**
   a. Listen to the conversation, then answer the questions.
   b. Your homework is to read the interview and fill in the blanks.
   c. Practice the conversation on page 26 in the book. Work in pairs.

9. **Assign homework for tomorrow.**
   a. For our next class, please read the text on page 16 and answer the questions.
   b. Next time, don't forget to bring your homework.
   c. Your assignment is due next class.

10. **A student came to class without his homework. You say:**
    a. Complete the activity on page 40 in the workbook.
    b. Next time, don't forget to bring your homework.
    c. Next time, don't forget to bring your book.

REFLECT

Think about what you learned in this lesson. Write five phrases you practiced.

Phrases for Assigning Homework

Now rate your confidence using these phrases. Put a check below your confidence level.

not confident	a little confident	somewhat confident	very confident

LESSON 9 DISMISSING THE CLASS

PREVIEW

You can dismiss your class in English.

In Lesson 9, you will:

- prepare to finish the lesson.
- announce when class is over.
- say goodbye at the end of class.
- respond to students when they say goodbye.

Language to Know

area	desk	dismiss	evening	put away	table	weekend

What Do You Know?

Write the phrases you know for dismissing the class in English. One example is below:

Goodbye.

Rate your confidence using these phrases. Put a check below your confidence level.

not confident	a little confident	somewhat confident	very confident

LEARN 1

A. Here are some phrases for dismissing class. Listen and repeat. 1.24

Dismissing the Class

Goodbye.

See you tomorrow.

Class is finished.

You can go now.

Have a good afternoon.

Good job today.

It's time to clean up.

Please clean up your area.

Please put away your books.

You can finish this exercise at home.

B. There are many substitutions for these phrases. Listen and repeat. 1.25

Phrases	Substitutions
Goodbye.	Bye.
See you tomorrow.	See you Friday/next week/next Friday.
Have a good afternoon.	Have a good evening/weekend.
It's time to clean up.	It's time to put away your books.
Please clean up your area.	Please clean up the desks/tables.
Please put away your books.	Please put your books away.
You can finish this exercise at home.	You can finish this activity for next class.

LEARN 2

Read the conversation, and watch the video. Listen to the teacher dismiss her class. ▶ 1.8

Ms. Silva: Did everyone finish?
Class: No.
Ms. Silva: It's OK. You can finish this activity at home. Good job today. Yes, Pedro?
Pedro: Can we go?
Ms. Silva: It's time to clean up. Please put away your books. Pedro, can you help me?
Pedro: Yes.
Ms. Silva: OK, everyone, Pedro will collect your papers.
Ms. Silva: Class is finished. You can go now.
Pedro: Goodbye, Ms. Silva.
Ms. Silva: Bye, Pedro. Have a good afternoon.

PRACTICE 1

Write the words in the correct order to make a sentence.

1. today/job/Good ______
2. clean up/time /It's/to ______
3. books/Put away/your ______
4. is/Class/finished ______
5. next/you/See/week ______
6. now/go/You/can ______
7. good/a/weekend/Have ______
8. your/clean up/Please/area ______
9. Monday/next/you/See ______
10. Have/afternoon/good/a ______

PRACTICE 2

Fill in the blanks with the words and phrases. Use the correct punctuation.

goodbye	good job	see	you can finish

1. **Ms. Silva:** ______ today, Ana. You worked very hard.
Ana: Thank you. ______ you tomorrow.

good	goodbye	good job	see

2. Pedro: ________________, Ms. Silva!

Ms. Silva: Goodbye, Pedro! Have a ________________ afternoon.

Pedro: Thank you. You, too!

can	finished	goodbye	see

3. Ana: ________________ we go?

Ms. Silva: Yes, Ana. Class is ________________.

Ana: Thank you! Bye.

class	good job	see you	weekend

4. Ms. Silva: Goodbye. ________________ Monday.

Pedro: Bye! Have a good ________________, Ms. Silva.

evening	finish	put away	time

5. Ms. Silva: Ana, where is your bag?

Ana: Here.

Ms. Silva: OK. It's ________________ to clean up. Please ________________ your books.

REFLECT

Think about what you learned in this lesson. Write five phrases you practiced.

Phrases for Dismissing the Class

Now rate your confidence using these phrases. Put a check below your confidence level.

not confident	a little confident	somewhat confident	very confident

LESSON 10 REVIEW B

1 Fill in the blanks with the words and phrases. Then practice the teacher's lines.

Don't forget to study	some announcements	there's a change	visitor	write

Teacher: I have ______________ to make. Does everyone have their notebook?

Students: Yes.

Teacher: OK. Please listen carefully and ______________ it down. We will have a test next week.
Student: What day?

Teacher: On Tuesday. ______________ pages 10 to 12.
Student: Can you repeat that?

Teacher: Remember to study pages 10 to 12. Also, on Friday, ______________ in the schedule. We will have lunch early.

Student: Why?
Teacher: We're going to have a ______________.

2 Read and listen to the model sentences. Practice saying the sentences aloud. 1.26

1. Good job today. You can go now. See you tomorrow.
2. For our next class, please listen to the dialog and then answer the questions.
3. Your assignment is on page 19 in your textbook. Please write it down.
4. Remember that we have a quiz on Tuesday. Study the vocabulary on page 10.
5. It's time to put away your books. Class is finished. Have a good afternoon.

3 Read the conversation. Choose the best response.

1. **Teacher:** I have an announcement to make. There will be a class trip next week.
   Student: Where are we going?
   Teacher: ______________
   a. At 2:00 today.
   b. To the zoo.
   c. Today is Monday.
   d. Next Tuesday.

2. **Teacher:** Please listen carefully. We are going to do a report about sports.
   Student: When is it due?
   Teacher: ______________
   a. Please work with a partner.
   b. Please do a report about sports.
   c. You should finish by April 10.
   d. Complete Exercise B on page 20.

3. **Teacher:** I have something to tell you. There will be a test next Friday.
   Student: What do we have to study?
   Teacher: ______________________
   a. Your homework is due next class.
   b. The test will take until the end of class.
   c. Review pages 9 and 10 in your textbook.
   d. Don't forget about the concert tonight.

4. **Teacher:** Please listen carefully. There's a schedule change tomorrow.
   Student: Why?
   Teacher: ______________________
   a. It's time to put away your books.
   b. Please give this invitation to your parents.
   c. Write your name on your paper.
   d. A visitor is coming to talk about books.

5. **Teacher:** Your homework is to listen to the dialog and complete the exercise on page 8.
   Student: Is the homework for our next class?
   Teacher: ______________________
   a. Next time, don't forget to bring your book.
   b. Yes. Your assignment is due tomorrow.
   c. Your homework is on Chapter 9.
   d. Next week we will visit a museum.

UNIT 2 RESEARCH BRIEF
MANAGING THE CLASSROOM: Setting Up Learning Opportunities

The language and routines in Unit 2 will help you set up or create learning opportunities[1] for students. This is an important part of managing your classroom. Here is some research supporting this unit.

What does it mean to manage the classroom?

Classroom management refers to the routine actions teachers take to create opportunities for learning. Some examples include giving clear directions, checking that students understand directions, and encouraging student participation. These teachers anticipate[2] what information students need to have to participate in class. These strategies also motivate students to participate in classroom activities. Together, these strategies create a classroom environment that helps learning.

Why is classroom management important for student learning?

Students need a learning environment where teaching is smooth and continuous. Students learn best when the teacher's expectations are clear. When instruction is disorganized or interrupted, learning is difficult for students. Classroom teachers understand this and prevent[3] classroom disruptions.[4] Preventing disruptions is more effective than reacting[5] to them. A classroom where students can concentrate and participate in the lesson creates more opportunities for learning.

A research study

HOW DO TEACHERS MAINTAIN ON-TASK BEHAVIOR?

Jacob Kounin was an educational researcher who studied classroom management. He changed the focus of classroom management research from "good behavior" to "student engagement." He used videos of classroom instruction to describe the behavior of teachers and students, and he found that effective teachers anticipated student misbehavior and prevented it.

Kounin (1973) identified what he called "with-it-ness." He defined with-it-ness as a characteristic of teachers who noticed small changes in students' emotions or behavior. Kounin found that these "with-it" teachers acted before students disrupted instruction. He also found that the with-it teachers were effective at maintaining students' focus on classroom activities. Later studies have supported Kounin's findings, and researchers continue to see student engagement as an important part of classroom management.

---

[1] opportunity: a chance
[2] anticipate: to expect, plan, predict
[3] prevent: to stop from happening
[4] disruption: disturbance
[5] react: to act in response to something

Research questions and findings

Below are some questions researchers have asked about how to create opportunities for learning. Findings of these studies are listed after each question.

1. **How do teachers effectively manage the classroom?**
   Two large analyses (Korpershoek, Harms, de Boer, van Kuijk, & Doolard, 2016; Marzano & Pickering, 2003) found that teachers take specific actions. They

   a. develop rules and procedures.

   b. anticipate and directly address student behavior (i.e., Kounin's "with-it-ness").

   c. build warm, caring relationships with students.

   d. help students develop self-control.

   e. help students build empathy[6] for other students and improve social skills.

2. **How do language teachers motivate students and encourage student participation?**
   Language teachers use a variety of strategies. They

   a. provide feedback that motivates students (Guilloteaux & Dörnyei, 2008; Walsh & Li, 2013).

   b. protect the students' self-esteem[7] (Guilloteaux & Dörnyei, 2008).

   c. create a supportive classroom environment (Cheng & Dörnyei, 2007).

   d. help students see how materials connect to their lives (Cheng & Dörnyei, 2007).

   e. ask guided questions and/or ask for more information (Walsh & Li, 2013).

[6] empathy: the ability to understand feelings
[7] self-esteem: confidence

UNIT 2 MANAGING THE CLASSROOM: ACTIVITIES

LESSON 1 USING CLASSROOM MATERIALS

PREVIEW

You can give instructions and answer questions about classroom materials in English.

In Lesson 1, you will:
- instruct students to use classroom materials.
- respond to student questions about classroom materials.

Language to Know

blackboard	bottom	middle	turn in	whiteboard
borrow	flashcard	smartboard	turn over	

What Do You Know?

Do you know these phrases for talking about classroom materials? Write *K* if you know the phrase. Write *DK* if you do not know the phrase.

__________ Do you have a pencil?

__________ Please take out your book.

__________ Open your books.

__________ Please turn to page 27.

__________ Please look at the handout.

__________ Write your name on your paper.

__________ Hand in your papers.

__________ The exercise is at the top of page 28.

LEARN 1

A. Here are some phrases for using classroom materials. Listen and repeat. 2.1

Using Classroom Materials

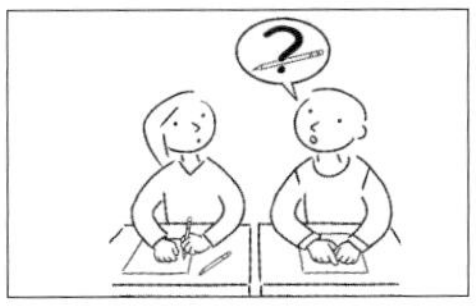

Do you have a pencil?

Does everyone have their books?

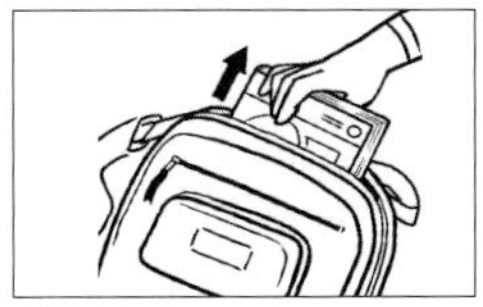

Please take out your book.

Open your books.

Please turn to page 27.

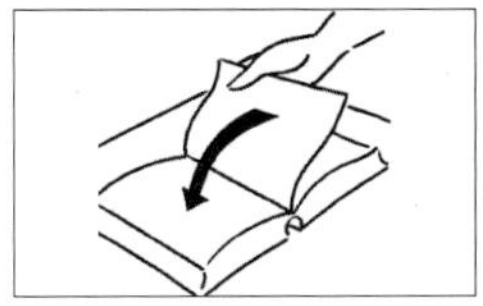

Please turn the page.

Please look at the handout.

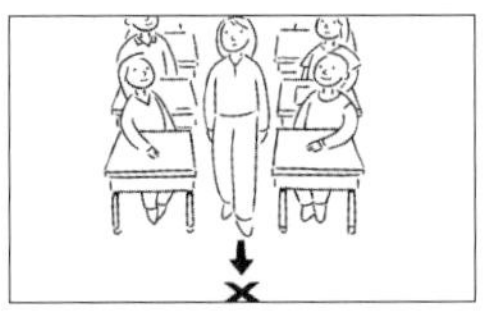

Please come to the front.

Close your books.

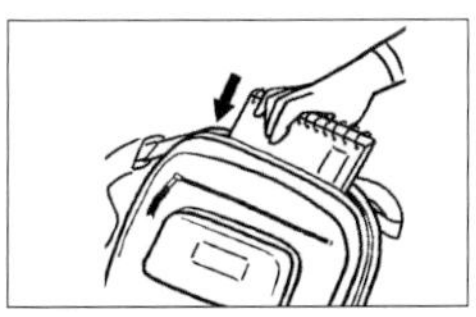

Put away your notebooks.

Write your name on your paper.

Turn over your paper.

Hand in your papers.

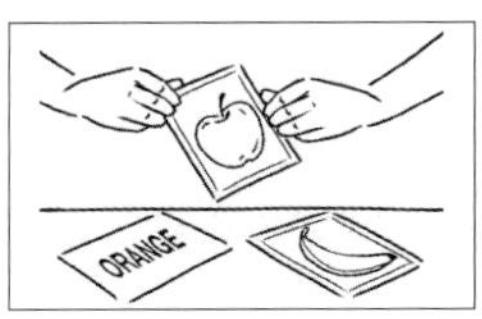

Use the flashcards to review.

Use the dictionary to check new words.

The exercise is at the top of page 28.

Do the exercise at the bottom of page 23.

Read the example in the middle of page 15.

B. There are many substitutions for these phrases. Listen and repeat. 2.2

Phrases	Substitutions
Do you have a pencil?	Do you have your book?
Does everyone have their books?	Does everyone have a pencil?
Please take out your book.	Please take out your notebook/dictionary.
Please look at the handout.	Please look at the worksheet/blackboard/ whiteboard/smartboard.
Please come to the front.	Please come to the board.
Put away your notebooks.	Put away your books/pencils.
Write your name on your paper.	Write the date on your paper.
Use the flashcards to review.	Use the flashcards to study/practice.
The exercise is at the top of page 28.	The dialog is at the top of page 28. The example is at the bottom of page 28. The text is in the middle of page 28.
Do the exercise at the bottom of page 23.	Do the exercise at the top of page 23. Do the exercise in the middle of page 23.
Read the example in the middle of page 15.	Read the dialog/text in the middle of page 15. Read the example at the top of page 15. Read the example at the bottom of page 15.

LEARN 2

Read the conversation, and watch the video. Listen to the teacher instruct students to use classroom materials. 2.1

Ms. Choi: Let's begin. Does everyone have their books? Please open your books to page 10.

Sangwoo: What page?

Ms. Choi: Page 10, Sangwoo. Is everyone ready?

Class: Yes.

Ms. Choi: Sangwoo, please read the words at the top of the page.

Sangwoo: Apple, orange, banana, strawberry, grape.

Ms. Choi: Good job. Mirae, please come to the front. Please write "apple." Look at the board, everyone. Is that right?

Class: Yes.

Ms. Choi: Good job, Mirae. OK, class. Do the exercise at the top of page 11.

PRACTICE 1

Choose the correct answer.

1. **Does __________ have their books?**
   a. everyone
   b. all
   c. you
   d. every

2. **Please take __________ your notebooks.**
   a. over
   b. in
   c. out
   d. from

3. **Please __________ at the worksheet.**
   a. see
   b. watch
   c. look
   d. work

4. **Open your books __________ page 27.**
   a. at
   b. on
   c. in
   d. to

5. **__________ the flashcards to practice.**
   a. Use
   b. Open
   c. Come to
   d. Hand in

6. **__________ over your paper.**
   a. Open
   b. Turn
   c. See
   d. Do

7. **Put __________ your pencils.**
   a. away
   b. in
   c. on
   d. over

8. **__________ in your papers.**
   a. Write
   b. Do
   c. Have
   d. Hand

9. **Do the exercise __________ the top of the page.**
   a. by
   b. over
   c. at
   d. in

10. **Read the words __________ of page 15.**
    a. at the middle
    b. in the middle
    c. in the bottom
    d. in the top

PRACTICE 2

Fill in the blanks with the phrases.

Does everyone have their books	Please turn to page 27	the dictionary
Read the example at the bottom of page 27	Open your books	

Ms. Choi: ______________________________?
Class: Yes, we do.

Ms. Choi: Good. ______________________________.
Sangwoo: What page?
Ms. Choi: ______________________________. Mirae, please read the example.
Mirae: Where's the example?

Ms. Choi: ______________________________.
Mirae: "I take the bus to school."

Ms. Choi: Very good, Mirae. Class, continue reading the sentences. Use ______________________________ to check new words.

do the exercise in the middle	please look at the handout	Write your name on your paper
hand in your papers	turn over	

Ms. Choi: OK, class, ______________________________. Sangwoo, do you have the handout?
Sangwoo: No, I don't.

Ms. Choi: Here you are. ______________________________.
Sangwoo: Can I borrow a pencil?

Ms. Choi: Yes, Sangwoo. Everyone, please ______________________________ of the handout. When you are finished, ______________________________ your papers.
Mirae: Do we hand it in?

Ms. Choi: Please do not ______________________________. I will collect them.

PRACTICE 3

Read the situation. Choose the correct answer. Then practice saying the answer aloud.

1. **You are preparing to do a reading activity. You say:**
   a. Close your books.
   b. Put away your notebooks.
   c. Please take out your book.

2. **You have just finished reading. You say:**
   a. Open your books to page 95.
   b. Close your books.
   c. Does everyone have a pencil?

3. **Students just opened their books. Next you say:**
   a. Use the flashcards to practice.
   b. Turn over your paper.
   c. Do the exercise at the bottom of page 23.

4. **You want students to study vocabulary for a quiz. You say:**
   a. Read the example at the bottom of page 10.
   b. Use the dictionary to check spelling.
   c. Use the flashcards to review.

5. **As you give each student a handout, you say:**
   a. Hand in your papers.
   b. Write your name on your paper.
   c. Please turn the page.

6. **A student has his book open to page 25. The exercise you want him to do is on page 26. You say:**
   a. Close your book.
   b. Please turn the page.
   c. Please turn to page 25.

7. **You have just given each student a worksheet. You say:**
   a. Please look at the handout.
   b. Please come to the board.
   c. Hand in your papers.

8. **You are preparing to give a quiz. You say:**
   a. Put away your notebooks.
   b. Open your books to page 15.
   c. Please come to the front.

9. **Time is up and you want the students' tests. You say:**
   a. Does everyone have their books?
   b. Please look at the handout.
   c. Hand in your papers.

10. **A student has finished her quiz, but you plan to collect them when everyone finishes. You say:**
    a. Put away your notebook.
    b. Read the example at the top of the page.
    c. Turn over your paper.

REFLECT

Think about what you learned in this lesson. Write five phrases you practiced.

Phrases for Using Classroom Materials

Now rate your confidence using these phrases. Put a check below your confidence level.

not confident	a little confident	somewhat confident	very confident

LESSON 2 TEACHING CLASSROOM LANGUAGE

PREVIEW

You can show students how to ask for help in English. This will encourage students to use English on their own.

In Lesson 2, you will:

- help students use English in class.
- explain how to ask for help.
- respond to student questions about classroom language.

Language to Know

bathroom	mean	repeat	slowly	spell	understand

What Do You Know?

Do you know these phrases for teaching classroom language? Write *K* if you know the phrase. Write *DK* if you do not know the phrase.

__________ Please ask me in English.

__________ Repeat after me, please.

__________ You can say, "Can you repeat that, please?"

__________ You can say, "Can you speak more slowly?"

__________ You can say, "Can you write that on the board?"

__________ You can say, "May I go to the bathroom, please?"

__________ When you don't understand, ask: "What does it mean?"

LEARN 1

A. Here are some phrases for teaching classroom language. Listen and repeat. 2.3

Teaching Classroom Language

Please ask me in English.

Repeat after me, please.

You can say, "May I have a pencil, please?"

You can say, "Can you repeat that, please?"

You can say, "Can you speak more slowly?"

You can say, "Can you write that on the board?"

You can say, "May I go to the bathroom, please?"

When you don't understand, ask: "What does it mean?"

When you want to know a word, say: "How do you say this in English?"

When you want to write a word, say: "How do you spell that?"

B. There are many substitutions for these phrases. Listen and repeat. 2.4

Phrases	Substitutions
You can say, "May I have a pencil, please?"	You can say, "May I have a book, please?"
When you don't understand, ask: "What does it mean?"	When you don't understand, say: "What does it mean?"

LEARN 2

Read the conversation, and watch the video. Listen to the teacher teach classroom language. ▶ 2.2

Ms. Choi: These are important questions. When you don't understand, please ask me in English. You can say, "Can you speak more slowly?" Repeat after me: "Can you speak more slowly?"

Class: "Can you speak more slowly?"

Ms. Choi: Good. When you want to write a word, say: "How do you spell that?" Repeat, please. "How do you spell that?"

Class: "How do you spell that?"

Ms. Choi: Very good. Mirae, do you have a question?

Mirae: Yes. Can you speak more slowly?

PRACTICE 1

Choose the correct answer.

1. **Please ______________ in English.**
   a. after me
   b. ask me
   c. you say
   d. can say

2. **You can say, "______________ speak more slowly?"**
   a. Repeat after
   b. Please ask
   c. Can you
   d. How do

3. **Repeat ______________, please.**
   a. after me
   b. does it
   c. when you
   d. can say

4. **When you ______________, ask: "What does it mean?"**
   a. ask me in English
   b. don't understand
   c. repeat after me
   d. write a word

5. **You can say, "May I ______________, please?"**
   a. understand that
   b. speak more slowly
   c. repeat that
   d. have a pencil

6. **When you want to ______________ a word, say: "How do you spell that?"**
   a. have
   b. repeat
   c. ask
   d. write

7. **You can say, "May I ______________ to the bathroom, please?"**
   a. go
   b. have
   c. get
   d. do

8. **You can ask, "Can you ______________ on the board?"**
   a. ask me
   b. repeat that
   c. write that
   d. say that

9. **When you want to ______________ a word, say: "How do you say this in English?"**
   a. go to
   b. repeat
   c. have
   d. know

10. **If you forget your book, you can say, "May I ______________, please?"**
   a. have a book
   b. have a pencil
   c. go to the bathroom
   d. read the book

PRACTICE 2

Fill in the blanks with the phrases.

can say	don't understand	on the board	repeat after	write
Can you	it mean	May I have	please ask	you spell

Ms. Choi: Let's review the worksheet. If you have a question, ______________ me in English. Sangwoo, do you have your worksheet?
Sangwoo: Worksheet?

Ms. Choi: It's OK. When you ______________, say, "What does ______________ ?"
Sangwoo: ______________ speak more slowly?

Ms. Choi: Yes. I said that you ______________, "What does it mean?" Everyone ______________ me, please. "What does it mean?"
Class: "What does it mean?"

Ms. Choi: Yes, Mirae?
Mirae: Write, please.

Ms. Choi: You can say, "Can you ______________ that ______________?" or "How do ______________ that?"
Mirae: How do you spell that? Oh, I want.

Ms. Choi: Do you need a pencil? You can say, "______________ a pencil, please?"

REFLECT

Think about the phrases you learned in this lesson. Write five phrases you practiced.

Phrases for Teaching Classroom Language

Now rate your confidence using these phrases. Put a check below your confidence level.

not confident	a little confident	somewhat confident	very confident

LESSON 3 DIRECTING STUDENTS

PREVIEW

You can give directions for classroom activities in English. You can use short phrases that are easy for students to understand.

In Lesson 3, you will:

- ask students to sit down and stand up.
- direct students to move around the classroom.
- prepare students for the next activity or break.
- respond to student questions about directions.

Language to Know

lunch	quiz	recess	sentence	test	word

What Do You Know?

Write the phrases you know for directing students in English. One example is below:

Please sit down.

Rate your confidence using these phrases. Put a check below your confidence level.

not confident	a little confident	somewhat confident	very confident

LEARN 1

A. Here are some phrases for directing students. Listen and repeat. 2.5

Directing Students

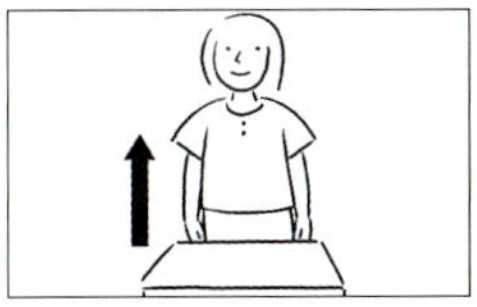

Stand up.

Line up.

Clean up.

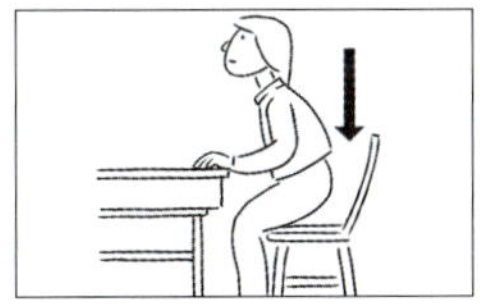

Please sit down.

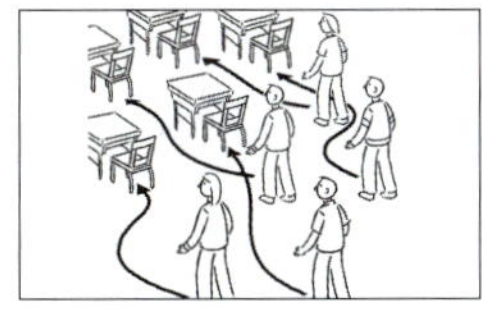

Go to your seats.

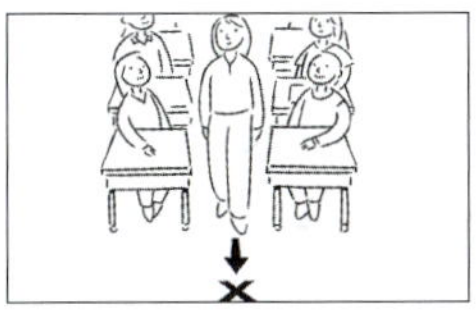

Please come to the front.

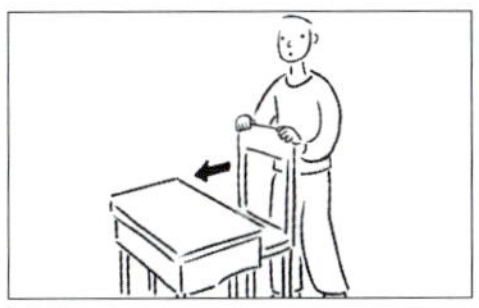

Push in your chairs.

Please speak louder.

Copy the words from the board.

Get ready for lunch.

B. There are many substitutions for these phrases. Listen and repeat. 2.6

Phrases	Substitutions
Please come to the front.	Please come to the board.
Copy the words from the board.	Copy the paragraph from the board. Copy the sentences from the board.
Get ready for lunch.	Get ready for recess/the quiz/the test.

LEARN 2

Read the conversation, and watch the video. Listen to the teacher direct her students. 2.3

Ms. Choi: All right, everyone go to your seats, please.
Sangwoo: What do I do? What should I do?
Ms. Choi: Sangwoo, please go to your seat. Mirae and Sangwoo, please stand up. Read the conversation for the class.
Mirae: Do you like to play tennis?
Ms. Choi: Please speak louder, Mirae.
Mirae: Do you like to play tennis?
Sangwoo: Yes, I do. How about you?
Mirae: No, I don't.
Ms. Choi: Very good. Please sit down. OK, good job, everyone. Now, please get ready for lunch. Line up and please be quiet.
Sangwoo: Where do I go?
Ms. Choi: Please line up, Sangwoo.

PRACTICE 1

Fill in the blanks with the words and phrases.

come to	line up	push in	recess	sit down
Copy	louder	ready	seats	stand up

1. It's time to begin class. Go to your ______________.
2. Please remember to ______________ your chairs.
3. It's 12:15 PM. Get ______________ for lunch.
4. Please ______________ and read number 3 for the class.
5. Class is finished. Please ______________ at the door.
6. Ana, please ______________ the board and write the answers.
7. This is your homework. ______________ the sentences from the board.
8. I can't hear you. Please speak ______________.
9. Sangwoo, where are you going? Please go to your desk and ______________ in your chair.
10. Get ready for ______________. Please wear your coats. It's cold today.

PRACTICE 2

Read the situation. Choose the correct answer. Then practice saying the answer aloud.

1. **You cannot hear what your student is saying. You say:**
   a. Line up.
   b. Please speak louder.
   c. Get ready for the test.

2. **You want students to take everything off their desk. You say:**
   a. Stand up.
   b. Please sit down.
   c. Get ready for the test.

3. **You want students to write down what is on the board. You say:**
   a. Copy the sentences from the board.
   b. Please come to the board.
   c. Get ready for the quiz.

4. **First, you ask a student to stand up. Then you say:**
   a. Please sit down.
   b. Please come to the front.
   c. Go to your seat.

5. **You want a student to write her sentence for the class to see. You say:**
   a. Stand up and come to the board.
   b. Please speak louder.
   c. Push in your chair.

6. **You are ready to begin class. You say:**
   a. Get ready for recess.
   b. Push in your chairs and stand up.
   c. Please go to your seats and sit down.

7. **The lesson is over. You say:**
   a. Please speak louder.
   b. Please come to the front.
   c. Clean up and get ready for recess.

8. **You are getting students ready to go to lunch. You say:**
   a. Please come to the front and line up.
   b. Please copy the paragraph from the board.
   c. Go to your seats and sit down.

9. **You want students to sit down. You say:**
   a. Line up and get ready for recess.
   b. Go to your seats and get ready for the quiz.
   c. Clean up and get ready for lunch.

10. **You want students to go to their seats and write. You say:**
   a. Go to your seats and speak louder.
   b. Sit down and get ready for lunch.
   c. Please sit down and copy the sentences from the board.

REFLECT

Think about what you learned in this lesson. Write five phrases you practiced.

Phrases for Directing Students

Now rate your confidence using these phrases. Put a check below your confidence level.

not confident	a little confident	somewhat confident	very confident

LESSON 4 GIVING TEST AND QUIZ INSTRUCTIONS

PREVIEW

You can give instructions for tests and quizzes in English.

In Lesson 4, you will:

- explain materials for a test or quiz.
- give time limits for a test or quiz.
- direct students during a test or quiz.
- respond to questions about instructions.

Language to Know

aloud	clear	eraser	pay attention	put down
check	desk	instruction	put away	quiet

What Do You Know?

Write the phrases you know for giving test and quiz instructions in English. One example is below:

Please be quiet.

Rate your confidence using these phrases. Put a check below your confidence level.

not confident	a little confident	somewhat confident	very confident

LEARN 1

A. Here are some phrases for giving test and quiz instructions. Listen and repeat. 2.7

Giving Test and Quiz Instructions

Now we're going to have a quiz on family words.

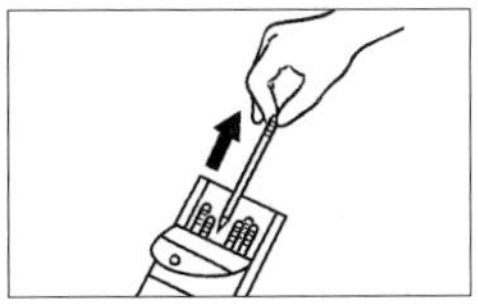

You need a pencil.

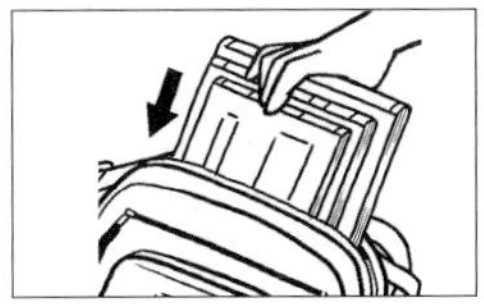

Put away your books.

Clear your desks.

Please be quiet.

I'm going to read the instructions aloud.

Pay attention to the instructions.

Remember to read the instructions carefully.

Write your name on the test.

You may use your dictionaries.

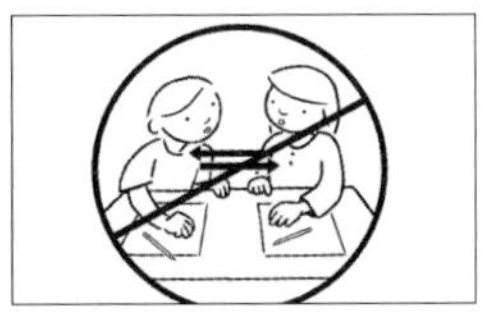

Do your own work.

No talking.

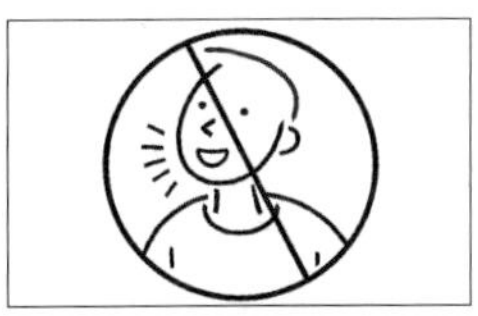

Don't talk.

You have five more minutes to finish the test.

Please finish up.

Time's up.

Stop writing.

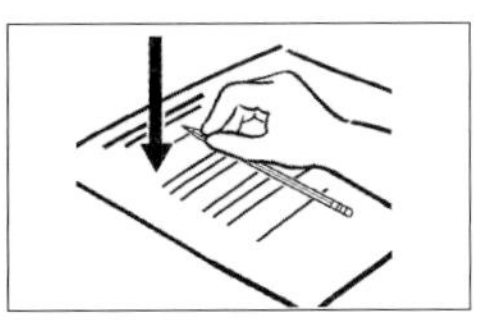

Put your pencils down.

Don't forget to check your work again.

B. There are many substitutions for these phrases. Listen and repeat. 2.8

Phrases	Substitutions
Now we're going to have a quiz on family words.	Now we're going to have a quiz on telling the time. Now we're going to have a test on past tense verbs.
You need a pencil.	You need an eraser.
Clear your desks.	Clear your tables.
I'm going to read the instructions aloud.	I'm going to read the instructions again.
Pay attention to the instructions.	Listen to the instructions.
You may use your dictionaries.	You may use your books. You may use your word lists.
You have five more minutes to finish the test.	You have five more minutes to complete the test. You have ten more minutes to finish the quiz.
Don't forget to check your work again.	Remember to check your work again. Don't forget to check your answers again.

LEARN 2

Read the conversation, and watch the video. Listen to the teacher give test instructions. 2.4

Ms. Choi: Please sit down. Put away your books and clear your desks. Now we're going to have a test on Unit 7. Did everyone study?

Class: Yes.

Ms. Choi: Good. You need a pencil. Write your name on the test. Remember to read the instructions carefully. Are there any questions?

Mirae: Yes. Can we use the dictionary?

Ms. Choi: Yes. You may use your dictionaries.

Sangwoo: I need a test, please.

Ms. Choi: Here. OK, let's begin. Please be quiet. No talking.

PRACTICE 1

Do you give these instructions at the beginning or end of a test? Write the instructions in the correct column.

Clear your tables. Please finish up. Stop writing. Time's up.	I'm going to read the instructions aloud. Put away your books. You need a pencil and an eraser.	Now we're going to have a test. Put your pencil down. You have one more minute.

Beginning of a Test	End of a Test

PRACTICE 2

Choose the correct sentence to continue the instructions.

1. **Please don't look at her paper.**

   ____

   a. Listen to the instructions
   b. Do your own work.
   c. You need a pencil.
   d. Time's up.

2. **I hear talking.** ____________________
   a. Please be quiet.
   b. Clear your tables.
   c. Please finish up.
   d. You have two more minutes.

3. **Time's up.** ____________________
   a. Pay attention to the instructions.
   b. No talking.
   c. Put your pencils down.
   d. You have 10 more minutes.

4. **You don't need your books.**

   ____

   a. Clear your desks.
   b. Please finish up.
   c. Please be quiet.
   d. Do your own work.

5. **Student:** How much time do we have?
   Teacher:____________________
   a. Please be quiet.
   b. Clear your desks.
   c. You need an eraser.
   d. You have 10 more minutes.

6. **Student:** I need a pencil.
   Teacher: ____________________
   a. Time's up. Stop writing. Pencils down.
   b. You have five more minutes to complete the test.
   c. Here you are. Write your name on your paper.
   d. Read the instructions carefully.

7. **Student:** What do I do first?
   Teacher: ______________________
   a. Write your name on the test.
   b. Time's up.
   c. You have five more minutes.
   d. Now we're going to take a test.

8. **Student:** Can we use the dictionary?
   Teacher: ______________________
   a. No, but you may use your word list.
   b. Remember to check your work.
   c. Write your name on the quiz.
   d. I'll read the instructions aloud.

9. **Student:** What do I do?
   Teacher: ______________________
   a. Put your pencils down.
   b. No talking.
   c. I'll read the instructions again.
   d. Now we're going to take a quiz.

10. **Student:** Can you read the instructions again?
   Teacher: ______________________
   a. No, but put away your books.
   b. No, but write your name on the test.
   c. Yes, now we're going to have a quiz.
   d. Yes, but please pay attention to the instructions.

REFLECT

Think about what you learned in this lesson. Write five phrases you practiced.

Phrases for Giving Test and Quiz Instructions

Now rate your confidence using these phrases. Put a check below your confidence level.

not confident	a little confident	somewhat confident	very confident

LESSON 5 REVIEW A

1 Fill in the blanks with the phrases. Then practice the teacher's lines.

10 minutes to complete the quiz	check new words	"What does it mean?"
carefully	have a quiz	Write your name

Teacher: We're going to ______________________. Does everyone have a pencil?
Class: Yes.

Teacher: ______________________ and the date. You have ______________________.
Student: Excuse me, teacher. I need a quiz, please.

Teacher: Here is a quiz. Read the instructions ______________________. You may use your dictionaries.
Student: Excuse me. "Dictionaries"?

Teacher: Yes. This is a dictionary. When you don't understand, ask: ______________________
Student: What does "dictionaries" mean?
Teacher: Dictionaries give the meanings of words. Use your dictionary to ______________________.

2 Read the conversation. Choose the best response.

1. **Teacher:** Please take out your book.
   Student: Which book?
   Teacher: ______________________
   a. Page 18 in your book.
   b. Please ask me in English.
   c. Put your books away.
   d. Your workbook, please.

2. **Teacher:** Write your name on your paper.
   Student: Where do I write my name?
   Teacher: ______________________
   a. At the top of the page.
   b. You need a pencil and an eraser.
   c. Write the date on your paper.
   d. Please come to the front.

3. **Teacher:** Use the flashcards to review and please be quiet.
   Student: What do I do?
   Teacher: ______________________
   a. Study silently.
   b. Ask in English.
   c. Finish up.
   d. Speak louder.

4. **Teacher:** Please look at the whiteboard. Copy the sentences from the board.
   Student: Where do I write the sentences?
   Teacher: ______________________
   a. You have 10 minutes to finish the quiz.
   b. Write the sentences in your notebook.
   c. When you finish, turn in your paper.
   d. Stop writing. Put your pencils down.

5. **Teacher:** Open your books. Turn to page 27. Look at the exercise at the top of the page.
   Student: Can you repeat that please?
   Teacher: ____________________
   a. When you want to write a word, say: "How do you spell that?"
   b. Turn the page. Read the instructions carefully.
   c. Look at the top of page 27 in your book.
   d. Please ask me in English. You can say: "What does it mean?"

3 Read and listen to the model sentences. Practice saying the sentences aloud. 2.9

1. Please stand up and come to the board.
2. Get ready for lunch. Line up. Please be quiet.
3. Time's up. Put your pencils down. Turn over your papers.
4. Please ask me in English. You can say, "May I have a pencil, please?"
5. Now we are going to have a test. Please be quiet. Pay attention to the instructions.

4 Write sentences to give instructions. Use the key words.

1. Give test instructions.
   time's up/writing ____________________
2. Direct students.
   clean/ready/lunch ____________________
3. Give quiz instructions.
   put away/notebooks/close/books ____________________
4. Explain how to use classroom materials.
   use flashcards/review/use dictionary/check/new words ____________________
   ____
5. Teach classroom language.
   ask me/English/You/say/may/go/bathroom ____________________
   ____

LESSON 6 CHANGING ACTIVITIES

PREVIEW

You can introduce new activities in English.

In Lesson 6, you will:
- get students' attention.
- move to a new activity.
- explain what students will do next.
- respond to questions on changing activities.

Language to Know

get started	move on	pay attention	start

What Do You Know?

Write the phrases you know for getting students' attention and moving to a new activity in English. Two examples are below:

Getting Students' Attention	Moving to a New Activity
Attention, please!	Now, we will…

Rate your confidence using these phrases. Put a check below your confidence level.

not confident	a little confident	somewhat confident	very confident

LEARN 1

A. Here are some phrases for getting students' attention. Listen and repeat. 2.10

Getting Students' Attention

OK!

All right.

Please listen.

Please pay attention.

Attention, please!

Can you pay attention, please?

B. Here are some phrases for moving to a new activity. Listen and repeat. 2.11

Moving to a New Activity

Let's get started.

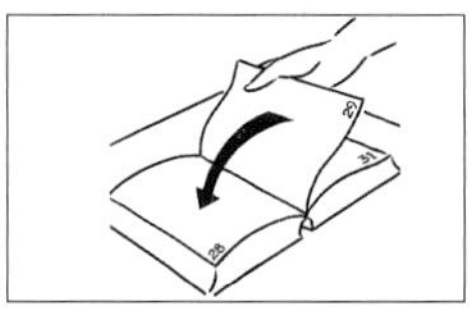

Turn to page 31.

OK, everybody. Let's start an exercise in Unit 5.

Let's look at the picture on page 37.

Now, let's move on to the next activity.

We will now start a different activity.

Now, we will learn something new.

C. There are many substitutions for these phrases. Listen and repeat. 2.12

Phrases	Substitutions
OK, everybody. Let's start an exercise in Unit 5.	OK, everybody. Let's start a game. OK, everybody. Let's start an activity on page 35.
Now, let's move on to the next activity.	Now, let's move on to the workbook.
Now, we will learn something new.	Now, we will start the quiz. Now, we will check the homework. Now, we will practice what we learned. Now, we are going to use the new vocabulary.

LEARN 2

Read the conversation, and watch the video. Listen to the teacher move to a new activity. ▶ 2.5

Ms. Choi: All right. Attention, please. Did everyone finish the worksheet?
Class: Yes.
Ms. Choi: Good. Mirae, can you help me?
Mirae: Sure.
Ms. Choi: Mirae, help me collect the worksheets. OK, everybody. Mirae will collect your worksheets. Now let's move on to the next activity. Does everyone have their textbooks?
Class: Yes.
Ms. Choi: Good. Let's get started. Please open your books.
Sangwoo: What page?
Ms. Choi: Turn to page 27. Let's look at the picture.
Mirae: Which picture?
Ms. Choi: Please look at the one at the bottom of the page.

PRACTICE 1

Fill in the blanks with the words.

get	learned	move	Please	Turn
going	look	pay	something	will

1. ______________ listen.
2. Please______________ attention.
3. Let's______________ started.
4. ______________ to page 30.
5. Now, we're going to learn ______________ new.
6. Now, we will practice what we ______________ .
7. Let's ______________ at the picture on page 38.
8. Now, let's______________ on to Unit 5.
9. Now, we're ______________ to check the homework.
10. We ______________ now start a different activity.

PRACTICE 2

Read the situation. Choose the correct answer. Then practice saying the answer aloud.

1. **You are ready to start a new unit. You say:**
   a. Let's start a game.
   b. Please listen. Let's move on to Unit 2.
   c. We will now start a different activity.

2. **You want to begin class with a game. You say:**
   a. OK, everybody. Let's start with a game.
   b. Let's get started. Turn to page 42.
   c. Can you pay attention please?

3. **You want students to look in their books. You say:**
   a. Let's look at the picture on page 30.
   b. Please listen. Let's get started.
   c. Now let's move on to the workbook.

4. **It is the beginning of class. You say:**
   a. Please close your books.
   b. Now, we are going to practice what we learned today.
   c. Let's start with an exercise in Unit 7.

5. **As you are giving students a book, you say:**
   a. Now we're going to read.
   b. Now, we will start the quiz.
   c. OK, everybody. Let's start a game.

6. **You want students to clear their desks. You say:**
   a. Please pay attention. Turn to page 31.
   b. All right. Can you pay attention, please?
   c. Now, we're going to start the quiz.

7. **You want to go over students' assignments at the beginning of class. You say:**
   a. Now, we're going to check the homework.
   b. All right. Now, let's move on to the workbook.
   c. Let's start an activity in Unit 7.

8. **You are giving students a test. You say:**
   a. Now, we will learn something new.
   b. Attention, please. Now, we will start the test.
   c. Now we are going to start the quiz.

9. **You want to review students' assignments. You say:**
   a. I want to assign your homework.
   b. I will give you homework on this lesson.
   c. All right. Now, we will check the homework.

10. **You have just finished teaching the material from Unit 5. You say:**
    a. Now, we will practice what we learned.
    b. OK, everybody. Let's start Unit 5.
    c. Let's get started. Turn to the first page of Unit 5.

REFLECT

Think about what you learned in this lesson. Write five phrases you practiced.

Phrases for Changing Activities

Now rate your confidence using these phrases. Put a check below your confidence level.

not confident	a little confident	somewhat confident	very confident

LESSON 7 DISCIPLINING

PREVIEW

You can give directions about classroom behavior in English.

In Lesson 7, you will:

- quiet students.
- keep students on task.
- get students' attention.

Language to Know

at a time	discipline	raise your hand	take turns
attraction	quiet	sit down	

What Do You Know?

Write the phrases you know for disciplining students in English. One example is below:

Please be quiet.

Rate your confidence using these phrases. Put a check below your confidence level.

not confident	a little confident	somewhat confident	very confident

LEARN 1

Here are some phrases for disciplining in English. Listen and repeat. 2.13

Disciplining

Please listen.

Please be quiet.

Please stop talking.

Please take turns.

One at a time.

Please pay attention.

Please get to work.

Please raise your hand.

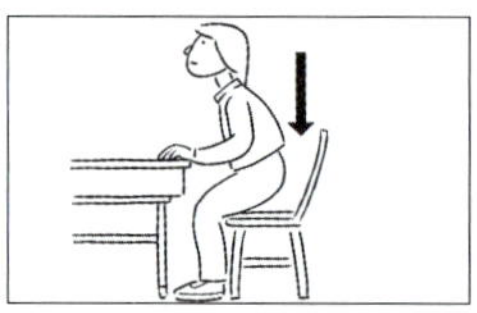

Sit down, please.

Please look at your own paper.

LEARN 2

Read the conversation, and watch the video. Listen to a teacher discipline her students. 2.6

Mrs. García: Class, please be quiet. You have some cards on your tables.

Alicia: Luis, do you have a pencil?

Mrs. García: Alicia, please stop talking.

Alicia: I'm sorry.

Mrs. García: Luis, sit down, please. I'm explaining the instructions.

Luis: Yes, Mrs. García. Um, what did you say?

Mrs. García: Please pay attention, Luis.

Luis: OK. I'm sorry.

Mrs. García: All right. Look at the cards on your tables. Look at the first picture. What is it? One at a time. Please raise your hand. Yes, Alicia?

Alicia: It's a horse.

Mrs. García: Good. It's a horse.

PRACTICE 1

Fill in the blanks with the words.

down	look	pay	raise	stop

1. Luis, this is a test. Please __________ at your own paper.
2. Do you have a question? Please __________ your hand.
3. Sit __________, please. It's time to begin class.
4. This is important information. Please __________ attention.
5. Please __________ talking and finish your work.

get	listen	one	quiet	turns

6. Please __________. I'm going to explain the game now.
7. Please come to the board __________ at a time.
8. I can't hear Alicia read. Please be __________.
9. Work together. Please take __________.
10. Luis, you did not finish. Please __________ to work.

PRACTICE 2

Choose *two* correct responses for each situation. Then practice saying the responses aloud.

1. **Students are talking. You want to begin the quiz. You say:**
   a. Please stop talking.
   b. Sit down, please.
   c. Please be quiet.
   d. One at a time.

2. **You asked the class a question. Many students call out answers. You say:**
   a. Please listen.
   b. One at a time.
   c. Please pay attention.
   d. Please raise your hand.

3. **You want to begin the lesson. Students are walking around the classroom. You say:**
   a. Sit down, please.
   b. Please listen.
   c. One at a time.
   d. Please go to your seats.

4. **You are explaining test instructions. Students are not listening. You say:**
   a. Please raise your hand.
   b. Please take turns.
   c. Please listen.
   d. Please pay attention.

5. **Students are playing a game. Several students want to go first. You say:**
   a. Please pay attention.
   b. Please take turns.
   c. One at a time.
   d. Please sit down.

6. **You are giving the lesson. Alicia is sleeping. You say:**
   a. Alicia, please pay attention.
   b. Alicia, please take turns.
   c. Alicia, please sit down.
   d. Alicia, please listen.

7. **The class is taking a quiz. Luis is looking at Alicia's paper. You say:**
   a. Please take turns.
   b. Do your own work.
   c. Please look at your own paper.
   d. Luis will collect your quizzes.

8. **The class is doing an activity. Some students are confused. You say:**
   a. Please raise your hand if you have a question.
   b. Please look at your own paper.
   c. Please stop talking and take out your homework.
   d. Please listen. I will read the instructions again.

9. **The class is taking a test. Two students are talking. You say:**
   a. Please take turns.
   b. Please look at the board.
   c. Please be quiet.
   d. Please stop talking.

10. **You are making an announcement. Students are not listening. You say:**
   a. Please listen.
   b. Please take turns.
   c. One at a time.
   d. Please pay attention.

REFLECT

Think about what you learned in this lesson. Write five phrases you practiced.

Phrases for Disciplining

Now rate your confidence using these phrases. Put a check below your confidence level.

not confident	a little confident	somewhat confident	very confident

LESSON 8 CHECKING STUDENT UNDERSTANDING

PREVIEW

You can check students' understanding in English.

In Lesson 8, you will:

- get students to ask questions.
- check that students understand the instructions.
- explain instructions for students.
- respond to student questions.

Language to Know

chart	example	explanation	repeat	review
clear	explain	instruction	reread	table

What Do You Know?

Do you know these phrases for checking student understanding? Write *K* if you know the phrase. Write *DK* if you do not know the phrase.

_______________ Is everything clear?

_______________ Do you understand the instructions?

_______________ I'll repeat the instructions.

_______________ Are there any questions?

_______________ Let me explain the chart again.

_______________ Let me give you an example.

_______________ Do you want another example?

_______________ So, what are we going to talk about?

LEARN 1

A. Here are some phrases for checking student understanding. Listen and repeat. 2.14

Checking Student Understanding

Is that clear?

Is everything clear?

Please read the instructions.

Do you understand the instructions?

I'll repeat the instructions.

I'll reread the explanation.

Let's review the instructions.

Are there any questions?

Do you have a question?

If you have a question, please raise your hand.

Let me explain the chart again.

Let me give you an example.

Are the examples clear?

Do you want another example?

...so what are we going to do?

...so what are you going to talk about?

B. There are many substitutions for these phrases. Listen and repeat. 2.15

Phrases	Substitutions
Do you understand the instructions?	Do you understand how to play the game? Do you understand what you have to do?
I'll reread the explanation.	I'll reread the instructions.
Let's review the instructions.	Let's review the instructions together.
Are there any questions?	Are there any questions on the exercise?
Do you have a question?	Do you have a question about the activity?
Let me explain the chart again.	Let me explain the table again.
Let me give you an example.	Let me repeat the example.
Do you want another example?	Do you want more examples?
So, what are we going to do?	So, what are you going to do? So, what are we going to do first? So, what are we going to do next?

LEARN 2

Read the conversation, and watch the video. Listen to the teacher check her students' understanding. ▶ 2.7

Mrs. García: Now, let's finish the worksheet. Alicia, do you have a question?

Alicia: I don't understand number 3.

Mrs. García: All right. Let's review the instructions. "First, look at the pictures on the worksheet. Then, write the words from the box under the pictures." So what are you going to do?

Luis: Write the words under the pictures.

Mrs. García: That's right. Is that clear, everyone?

Class: Yes, Mrs. García.

Mrs. García: So, what are you going to write under picture A? Alicia?

Alicia: "Bird."

Mrs. García: Right. Do you want another example?

PRACTICE 1

Choose the correct answer.

1. **Teacher:** Do you ______________________?
   Student: No, I don't understand.
   a. review
   b. understand
   c. question
   d. explain

2. **Student:** I don't understand Exercise 2.
   Teacher: Please ______________________ the instructions.
   a. do
   b. read
   c. raise
   d. understand

3. **Teacher:** The instructions are, "Talk to a partner about foods you like." So, what are you going to ______________________ about?
   Student: Foods.
   a. read
   b. talk
   c. do
   d. say

4. **Teacher:** Let's begin the quiz. Are there any ______________________?
   Student: Yes. May I have a pencil?
   a. examples
   b. explanations
   c. instructions
   d. questions

5. **Teacher:** Do you have ______________________?
   Student: Yes. What does "run" mean?
   a. instructions
   b. an explanation
   c. your textbook
   d. a question

6. **Teacher:** Let's read the questions next. So, what ______________________ to do next?
   Student: Read the questions.
   a. do we like
   b. are we being
   c. are we going
   d. are we doing

7. **Student:** I don't understand Exercise 3.
Teacher: Let me ______________________.
I'll write it on the board.
   a. give you an example
   b. have a question
   c. repeat the words
   d. raise your hand

8. **Student:** Can you explain again?
Teacher: Sure. I'll ______________________.
   a. begin the test
   b. reread the instructions
   c. ask a question
   d. work with a partner

9. **Student:** Teacher! What do we do?
Teacher: If you have a question, please ______________________.
   a. raise your hand
   b. come to the board
   c. write number 3
   d. give an example

10. **Teacher:** So, what are you going to do first?
Student: I'm sorry. I don't know.
Teacher: OK. ______________________ explain it again.
   a. Please
   b. Let me
   c. Don't
   d. You can

PRACTICE 2

Fill in the blanks with the sentences.

I'll reread the explanation.	If you have a question, please raise your hand.	
Is that clear, everyone?	Let me give you an example.	Let's review the instructions.

1. A student asks a question when it is not his turn. You say:
____

2. You want to say the instructions again. You say:
____

3. You want to ask if the class understands. You say:
____

4. Students don't understand an explanation. You say:
____

5. You need to show the class how to do something. You say:
____

Do you understand how to play the game?	Do you want another example?	
Let me explain the chart again.	So, what are we going to do?	What are we going to do first?

6. You want to be sure students understand what they are supposed to do. You say:

____

7. A student doesn't understand a chart. You say:

____

8. The first example isn't clear to students. You say:

____

9. You want to clarify the steps to an activity. You say:

____

10. Students are not playing a game correctly. You say:

____

REFLECT

Think about what you learned in this lesson. Write five phrases you practiced.

Phrases for Checking Student Understanding

Now rate your confidence using these phrases. Put a check below your confidence level.

not confident	a little confident	somewhat confident	very confident

LESSON 9 ENCOURAGING PARTICIPATION

PREVIEW

You can encourage students to be active in class in English. Students who are active in class learn more and gain confidence.

In Lesson 9, you will:

- ask for volunteers.
- ask for help with classroom tasks.
- encourage active participation.
- answer questions about participation.

Language to Know

encourage	help	louder	participate	pass out	read aloud	volunteer

What Do You Know?

Do you know these phrases for encouraging participation? Write *K* if you know the phrase. Write *DK* if you do not know the phrase.

__________ Please raise your hand.

__________ Please speak louder.

__________ Please read aloud.

__________ Who wants to volunteer?

__________ Who knows the answer?

__________ Do you want to try number 2?

__________ Do you know the answer to question 2?

__________ I need a volunteer to read the dialog.

LEARN 1

A. Here are some phrases for encouraging participation. Listen and repeat. 2.16

Encouraging Participation

Please raise your hand.

Please speak louder.

Please read aloud.

Who wants to volunteer?

Who knows the answer?

Luis, do you know 1?

Do you want to try number 2?

Alicia, do you know the answer to question number 2?

Luis, can you read, please?

Alicia, can you do question number 1 in the workbook?

I need a volunteer to read the dialog.

B. There are many substitutions for these phrases. Listen and repeat. 2.17

Phrases	Substitutions
Who wants to volunteer?	Who can help me? Who wants to read? Who wants to come to the board?
Who knows the answer?	Who knows the answer to question 3? Who knows the answer to question 3 in the workbook?
Luis, can you read, please?	Luis, can you write the answers on the board, please?
Alicia, can you do question number 1 in the workbook?	Alicia, can you do question number 1 on the worksheet?
I need a volunteer to read the dialog.	I need two volunteers to read the dialog. I need a volunteer to read the answers aloud. I need a volunteer to pass out papers. I need a volunteer to write the answers on the board.

LEARN 2

Read the conversation, and watch the video. Listen to the teacher ask for volunteers. ▶ 2.8

Mrs. García: Let's get started. I need two volunteers. Who wants to help me? Please raise your hands. Alicia, do you want to try?
Alicia: Yes.
Mrs. García: Please come to the board. One more volunteer. Who knows the answer to number 1?
Luis: What exercise?
Mrs. García: Exercise A in the workbook. Luis, can you read number 1? Alicia will write it on the board.
Luis: "The boy is running."
Mrs. García: Please speak louder.
Luis: "The boy is running."
Mrs. García: Very good. Who wants to try number 2?

PRACTICE 1

Fill in the blanks with the words and phrases.

aloud	can you	hand	knows	need
number	pass out	speak	wants to	help

1. I ____________ a volunteer.
2. Who can ____________ me?
3. Who ____________ the answer to number 1?
4. Please raise your ____________.
5. Please read ____________.
6. Please ____________ louder.
7. Alicia, do you know ____________ 3?
8. Who ____________ come to the board?
9. Luis, ____________ write number 2 on the board?
10. I need a volunteer to ____________ the papers.

PRACTICE 2

Read the situation. Choose the correct answer. Then practice saying the answer aloud.

1. **You want a student to write on the board. You say:**
   a. Who knows the answer?
   b. Who wants to write on the board?
   c. I can collect the homework.
   d. I need a volunteer to clean the board.

2. **You want a student to read to the class. You say:**
   a. Please speak louder.
   b. Please be quiet.
   c. Do you know number 2?
   d. Please read aloud.

3. **You need two students to help you. You say:**
   a. I need two volunteers.
   b. Do you know number 2?
   c. I need a volunteer.
   d. Do you want to try number 2?

4. **You want to check the answer to a quiz question. You say:**
   a. Do you have a question?
   b. Who wants to read?
   c. Who knows the answer?
   d. Now we are going to take a quiz.

5. **You can't hear the student's answer. You say:**
   a. Who knows the answer to question 3?
   b. Please speak louder.
   c. Can you write the answers on the board?
   d. Do you know the answer?

6. **You need help to give the class a worksheet. You say:**
   a. Does everyone have a worksheet?
   b. Who knows the answer to number 1?
   c. I need a volunteer to pass out the worksheets.
   d. Thank you for your help.

7. **You want a student to read number 3. You say:**
   a. I need three volunteers.
   b. Can you do number 3, please?
   c. Please speak louder.
   d. Who knows the answer to number 3?

8. **You need a student to pass out instructions to a game. You say:**
   a. Who wants to come to the board?
   b. I need two volunteers.
   c. Who can help me?
   d. Thank you for your help.

9. **Luis gave the incorrect answer for number 2. You say:**
   a. Alicia, do you know number 2?
   b. I need two volunteers.
   c. Luis, can you do number 2, please?
   d. Who wants to help me?

10. **Many students are shouting answers. You say:**
   a. Please read aloud.
   b. Who can help me?
   c. Who knows the answer?
   d. Please raise your hands.

REFLECT

Think about what you learned in this lesson. Write five phrases you practiced.

Phrases for Encouraging Participation

Now rate your confidence using these phrases. Put a check below your confidence level.

not confident	a little confident	somewhat confident	very confident

LESSON 10 MOTIVATING STUDENTS

PREVIEW

You can encourage and motivate students in English. Encouragement will help students focus and keep trying.

In Lesson 10, you will:

- give words of encouragement.
- help students with difficult tasks.
- motivate students to keep trying.
- respond to student comments.

Language to Know

difficult	encouragement	give up	motivate	take your time	trouble	worry

What Do You Know?

Write the words or phrases you know for motivating students in English. One example is below:

You can do it!

Rate your confidence using these phrases. Put a check below your confidence level.

not confident	a little confident	somewhat confident	very confident

LEARN 1

Here are some phrases for motivating students. Listen and repeat. 2.18

Motivating Students

Good job!

Keep trying!

Don't give up!

You can do it.

Just do your best.

You're doing great.

You can say that in English.

Try that in English.

Don't worry; take your time.

Don't worry; I'll explain it again.

LEARN 2

Read the conversation, and watch the video. Listen to the teacher encourage her students. 2.9

Mrs. García: Did everyone finish exercise B? Let's go over the answers.

Alicia: *Este...necesito más tiempo.*

Mrs. García: You can say that in English. Repeat: "I need more time."

Alicia: I need more time.

Mrs. García: Good job. OK. Don't worry; take your time. Luis, can you read question number 1?

Luis: "What is your fa..." Uh, I don't know the word.

Mrs. García: You're doing great. Don't give up. Just do your best.

Luis: "What is your favorite color?"

Mrs. García: Good job!

PRACTICE 1

Fill in the blanks with the words and phrases.

ask me	job	take	trying	your best

1. Don't worry; ___________ your time.
2. Good ___________!
3. Keep ___________.
4. Just do ___________.
5. You can ___________ in English.

explain it	give up	in English	You can	You're doing

6. Try that ___________, Luis.
7. Don't ___________.
8. ___________ do it.
9. Very good. ___________ great.
10. Don't worry; I'll ___________ again.

PRACTICE 2

Fill in the blanks with the words and phrases.

again	do it	give up	in English	say that in English
best	doing great	Good	Keep	time

1. **Student:** I finished the exercise.
   Teacher: ___________ job!
2. **Student:** I can't finish this activity.
   Teacher: ___________ trying. You can do it.
3. **Student:** I can't do this exercise.
   Teacher: It's OK. Just do your ___________.
4. **Student:** I am sorry. I am trying to do it.
   Teacher: Don't worry; take your ___________.
5. **Student:** Is this all right?
   Teacher: Yes. You're ___________.
6. **Student:** *Necesito más tiempo.*
   Teacher: You can ___________: "I need more time."
7. **Student:** I don't know what to do.
   Teacher: Don't worry; I'll explain it ___________ .
8. **Student:** This activity is difficult. I can't do it.
   Teacher: You can ___________. I will help you.
9. **Student:** I don't understand this.
   Teacher: Don't ___________. Keep trying.
10. **Student:** I only know how to say this in our language.
    Teacher: Try that ___________. You can do it.

REFLECT

Think about what you learned in this lesson. Write five phrases you practiced.

Phrases for Motivating Students

Now rate your confidence using these phrases. Put a check below your confidence level.

not confident	a little confident	somewhat confident	very confident

LESSON 11 REVIEW B

1 Fill in the blanks with the words and phrases. Then practice the teacher's lines.

Do you understand	instructions	next activity	speak louder
great	Let's review	read aloud	We are going to

Teacher: All right. Let's move to the ______________. ______________ to play a game.
Student: What game?

Teacher: Turn to page 31. Please read the ______________.
Student: What page?

Teacher: Thirty-one. OK, everyone. ______________ how to play the game?
Student: No, I don't understand.

Teacher: OK. ______________ the instructions together. Who wants to ______________?
Student: I can read. "Work in a group. Ask a question."

Teacher: Please ______________. You're doing ______________.

2 Fill in the blanks with the phrases.

Can you do question 1	Don't worry; take your time	Please be quiet
Can you pay attention, please	Is that clear	

1. **Teacher:** ______________.
   Students: OK. We will stop talking.

2. **Teacher:** You must write 10 sentences. ______________?
   Student: Yes, I understand now.

3. **Teacher:** ______________?
   Student: OK. I'm sorry. I will pay attention.

4. **Student:** This exercise is difficult!
   Teacher: ______________. Keep trying.

5. **Teacher:** ______________ in the workbook?
   Student: I don't understand the question. What do I do?

3 Read and listen to the model sentences. Practice saying the sentences aloud. 2.19

1. Attention, please! Let's get started.
2. Are there any questions? Please raise your hand.
3. I need a volunteer to pass out papers. Who wants to help me?
4. Don't give up. You can do it. Just do your best.
5. Do you understand how to play the game? Don't worry; I'll explain it again.

4 Write sentences to respond to students. Use the key words.

1. Teacher, we know the answer!

   raise/hands ______________________________

2. This exercise is difficult.

   do/great

   not/give up ______________________________

3. How do we do this?

   listen

   reread/explanation ______________________________

4. Can you explain again?

   give/example

   pay/attention ______________________________

5. We finished.

   job!

   now/move on/next activity

   turn/page 31 ______________________________

UNIT 3 RESEARCH BRIEF
UNDERSTANDING LESSON CONTENT: Planning Content for Student Understanding

The language and routines in Unit 3 help you practice planning and presenting different activities to help students understand the lesson content. The research below explains how and why this is important.

How do teachers plan and present activities for students?

It is important to plan and present activities carefully so that content is understandable to students. Using consistent[1] instructions and phrases for activities can help students know what to do. Teachers can also decide to use the textbook instructions and resources so that the activities are familiar to students. Textbooks support students as they learn. For example, textbooks often use consistent instructions and recycle or reuse activities through different units. Textbooks also include activities that give students chances to practice the four language skills. This helps students learn in different ways.

Why is it important for students to understand and use a variety of activities?

Students need practice to improve in a new language. If students do not understand the task the teacher asks them to do, it can be difficult for them to practice. If students are familiar with the instructions, it is easier for them to use the new language. Often when students can practice in groups or with partners before speaking in front of the whole class, they will be less anxious.[2]

Students also need chances to practice different language skills—reading, writing, speaking, and listening. Teachers should plan activities that include ways for students to hear or read language (input) and ways for students to write or speak language (output). When the teacher uses different input and output activities, the students have different ways of learning the material.

If content is too difficult for students, or if students don't know what they should do, they can become frustrated or anxious. These feelings can interfere[3] with their learning. Students who understand the task (what they are supposed to do) are more likely to enjoy learning more and learn more!

A research study

WHAT CAN TEXTBOOKS OFFER?

Using ideas from Ellis (2002), Vold (2020) explains different ways textbooks can help teachers teach language.

First, textbooks provide "explicit description." With grammar, for example, this means textbooks explain a grammar point directly. Second, textbooks include "data," which means they have examples with the new grammar point. Third, textbooks include "student activities" for students to practice the new language.

When planning activities, teachers should consider whether the textbook activities ask students to produce new language (output), understand new language (input), or make judgments about the language (identify errors). When students are asked to produce output, teachers can decide whether the activity is a drill (where students practice one grammar point) or communicative practice (where students use language to practice more freely).

[1] consistent: not changing; regular
[2] anxious: worried; nervous
[3] interfere: to block; get in the way of

Research questions and findings

Below are some questions researchers have asked about how to plan and present activities and use textbooks. Findings of these studies are listed after each question.

1. **What makes activities clear for students?**
   Activities are clear for students when

   a. tasks are familiar to students (DeKeyser, 2018).

   b. teachers use similar procedures (how to do the task) across different lessons. When students are familiar with the procedures, they ask for help less often and are more engaged in the content (Mackey, Kanganas, & Oliver, 2007).

   c. teachers know the lesson content well and explain it clearly and in different ways. This often means teachers have to plan carefully (Brosh, 1996).

   d. the language students hear or read (input) is slightly challenging for students but not too difficult for their level (Krashen, 1982).

2. **How can the teacher plan in ways that help students understand and use language activities?**
   Teachers can plan activities that

   a. include different ways for students to participate and use the four skills (listening, speaking, reading, and writing) together (Davies & Pearse, 2000).

   b. they choose specifically for their classroom in response to their students' interests and needs (Hall, 2016).

   c. allow for teacher–student and student–student interactions (Kumaravadivelu, 2003).

3. **How can textbooks help teachers plan and present activities?**
   Textbooks can help teachers to

   a. connect in class lessons with outside-of-class activities that use that grammar. Textbooks give examples of situations where a student might need to use a new grammar point (Vold, 2020).

   b. organize learning grammar and practice activities in a clear sequence (Kumaravadivelu, 2005).

   c. use a variety of modes (e.g., written examples, illustrations, and audio recordings) to present material (Liu & Qu, 2014).

   d. use a variety of ways to get students to practice the material (Tomlinson, 2011).

UNIT 3 UNDERSTANDING LESSON CONTENT

LESSON 1 UNDERSTANDING INSTRUCTIONS IN STUDENT MATERIALS

PREVIEW

You can read the instructions in student materials. This will help you prepare for the lesson.

In Lesson 1, you will:
- read instructions for listening and speaking activities.
- read instructions for reading and writing activities.

Language to Know

alternative	definition	line	own	table	true
correct	false	missing	paragraph	title	

What Do You Know?

Write the phrases you see in your students' textbooks. Two examples are below:

Instructions for Listening/Speaking	Instructions for Reading/Writing
Practice the conversation.	Fill in the blanks.

Rate your confidence using these phrases. Put a check below your confidence level.

not confident	a little confident	somewhat confident	very confident

LEARN 1

A. Here are some examples of instructions in student materials. Listen and repeat. 3.1

Instructions in Student Materials

Work in pairs.

Work with your partner.

Check your answers with a partner.

Check the following words in your dictionary.

Ask your partner about his or her family.

Fill in the blanks using the new vocabulary.

Practice the dialog.

Practice saying the vocabulary.

B. There are many substitutions for these phrases. Listen and repeat. 3.2

Phrases	Substitutions
Work in pairs.	Work in a group. Work in groups of three.
Work with your partner.	Work with a classmate.
Ask your partner about his or her family.	Ask your partner about your classmates.
Fill in the blanks using the new vocabulary.	Fill in the chart using the new vocabulary. Fill in the missing letters using the new vocabulary.
Practice the dialog.	Practice the conversation.
Practice saying the vocabulary.	Practice giving the date.

LEARN 2

A. Here are more examples of instructions in student materials. Listen and repeat. 3.3

Instructions in Student Materials

Give examples.

Underline the vocabulary.

Draw a picture in your notebook.

Circle the correct verb.

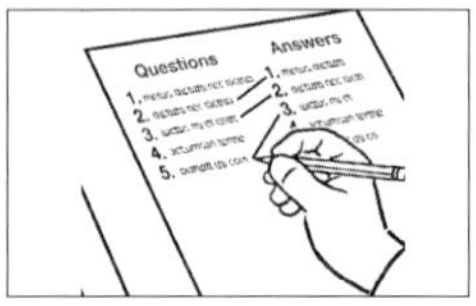

Match the questions with the answers.

Answer the questions.

Answer with complete sentences.

Choose one of the following activities.

B. There are many substitutions for these phrases. Listen and repeat. 3.4

Phrases	Substitutions
Underline the vocabulary.	Underline the verbs. Underline the correct word.
Match the questions with the answers.	Match the words with the definitions. Match the vocabulary with the pictures.
Answer the questions.	Answer *Yes* or *No*. Answer *True* or *False*.
Answer with complete sentences.	Answer with your own information.

LEARN 3

A. Here are some more examples of instructions in student materials. Listen and repeat. 3.5

Instructions in Student Materials

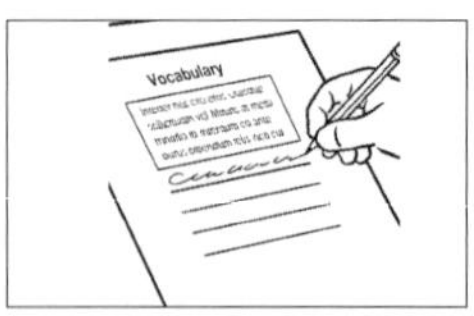

Use the vocabulary to write sentences.

Use the chart to answer the questions.

Repeat the sentences.

Guess the word.

Take turns reading the dialog.

Take notes about your partner.

Tell your partner about your family.

B. There are many substitutions for these phrases. Listen and repeat. 3.6

Phrases	Substitutions
Use the vocabulary to write the sentences.	Use the information to answer the questions.
Repeat the sentences.	Repeat the instructions/conversations.
Guess the word.	Guess the animal. Guess the name of the person.
Take turns reading the dialog.	Take turns writing the words. Take turns talking about your family.
Take notes about your partner.	Take notes on the reading.
Tell your partner about your family.	Tell your classmate about your family. Tell your partner about your photo. Tell the class about your weekend.

PRACTICE 1

Which instructions ask students to listen or speak? Which instructions ask students to read or write? Write the instructions in the correct column.

Ask your partner about his or her family.	Practice saying the vocabulary.
Circle the correct verb.	Practice the dialog.
Fill in the blanks using the missing letters.	Repeat the names.
Match the questions with the answers.	Underline the vocabulary.
Check the following words in your dictionary.	Use the chart to write the answers in your dictionary.

Students Listen or Speak	Students Read or Write

PRACTICE 2

Choose the correct answer.

1. **Ask your classmate ______________ about her family.**
   a. sentences
   b. answers
   c. questions
   d. notes

2. **Take ______________ on your partner's family.**
   a. notes
   b. definitions
   c. questions
   d. sentences

3. **Work in ______________ .**
   a. partners
   b. pairs
   c. classmates
   d. students

4. **Answer with ______________ sentences.**
   a. following
   b. own
   c. complete
   d. missing

5. **______________ the vocabulary with the definitions.**
   a. Match
   b. Answer
   c. Tell
   d. Take

6. **______________ turns reading the dialog.**
   a. Have
   b. Make
   c. Share
   d. Take

7. **Fill in the blanks ______________ the new vocabulary.**
   a. answering
   b. using
   c. working
   d. drawing

8. **Use the vocabulary ______________ write sentences.**
   a. for
   b. about
   c. to
   d. by

9. **Choose one ______________ the following activities.**
   a. on
   b. or
   c. in
   d. of

10. **Match the vocabulary ______________ the pictures.**
   a. with
   b. on
   c. at
   d. for

PRACTICE 3

Read the activity instructions. Then write *True* or *False*.

Instructions: Work with a partner. Take turns reading the text.

1. The students should work by themselves. ________
2. The students should read. ________

Instructions: Answer the questions about your school. Answer with complete sentences.

3. The students should use complete sentences. ________

Instructions: Match the pictures to the words. Check your answers with a partner.

4. The students should do an underlining activity. ________

Instructions: Check the following words in your dictionary. Practice saying the words with a partner.

5. The students have to check the meaning of the words. ________

Instructions: Ask your partner about his or her family. Take notes on your partner's family.

6. The students should work with a partner. ________

7. The students have to write. ________

Instructions: Work in groups of three. Fill in the blanks using the chart.

8. The students should complete a chart. ________

Instructions: Choose one of the following activities. Work in pairs.

9. The students have to do all of the activities. ________

Instructions: Use the vocabulary to write sentences. Underline the verbs in the sentences.

10. The students should listen. ________

REFLECT

Think about what you learned in this lesson. Write five phrases you practiced.

Instructions for Listening/Speaking	Instructions for Reading/Writing

Now rate your confidence using these phrases. Put a check below your confidence level.

not confident	a little confident	somewhat confident	very confident

LESSON 2 UNDERSTANDING LISTENING TEXTS IN STUDENT MATERIALS

PREVIEW

You can listen to audio texts in student materials. This helps you show students how to find answers.

In Lesson 2, you will:

- find answers to questions in listening texts.
- listen for answers in audio materials.

Language to Know

answer key	audio script	blank	chart	dictation	listening text	passage

What Do You Know?

How often do your students do these listening activities? Write each activity in one of the columns: *Often*, *Sometimes*, or *Rarely*.

do a dictation	listen and answer questions	listen and fill in the blanks
listen and match	listen and write in a chart	listen to a conversation
listen to a passage	listen to a song	listen to a story

Often	Sometimes	Rarely

LEARN 1

Read and listen to the audio script. Look at the answer key and notice the highlighted answers in the audio script. 3.7

Audio Script	Answer Key
Piñatas Birthdays are a lot of fun for most children. Around the world children do different things for their birthdays. In Mexico, they celebrate birthdays with piñatas. A piñata is a container filled with treats and candy. The birthday child's eyes are covered. Then the child hits the piñata with a stick until it breaks and all the candy falls out. All the children at the party run to get the candy. What do you do on your birthday?	**1.** What do children in Mexico use to celebrate their birthdays? a. A piñata is a container filled with treats and candy. (b.) In Mexico, children celebrate birthdays with piñatas. c. The birthday child's eyes are covered. d. The child hits the piñata with a stick until it breaks, and all the candy falls out. **2.** What does the birthday child do with the piñata? a. The birthday child's eyes are covered. b. All the children at the party run to get the candy. (c.) The child hits the piñata with a stick until it breaks, and all the candy falls out. d. Around the world, children do different things for their birthdays.

LEARN 2

Read and listen to the audio script. Look at the answer key and notice the highlighted answers in the audio script. 3.8

Audio Script		Answer Key
Alice:	Hi, William.	**1.** Does William want to join a club with Alice this year? Answer: **Yes**
William:	Hi, Alice.	
Alice:	Do you want to join a club with me this year?	
William:	Yes, I do.	**2.** Which club does William want to join? Answer: **The Sports Club**
Alice:	Which club do you want to join?	
William:	The Sports Club. How about you, Alice?	**3.** Which club does Alice want to join? Answer: **The Chess Club**
Alice:	I want to join the Chess Club. Do you like chess?	
William:	No, I don't. Do you like music?	**4.** What do Alice and William both like to do? Answer: **Singing and playing instruments**
Alice:	Yes, I like music. I like singing and playing instruments.	
William:	Me, too. Let's join the Music Club.	**5.** Which club are Alice and William going to join together? Answer: **The Music Club**
Alice:	OK!	

LEARN 3

Read and listen to the audio script. Look at the answer key and notice the highlighted answers in the audio script. 3.9

Audio Script	Answer Key
My name is Cassie. I live in an apartment. It has two bedrooms and one bathroom. It has a small kitchen and a large living room. It doesn't have a yard. My name is Tom. I live in a house. It has four bedrooms and two bathrooms. I have to share the bathroom with my sister. The house also has a yard. I like to play in my yard.	Listen to the people describe where they live. Circle *True* or *False*. Write the correct answer for false statements. **1.** Cassie lives in a house. True (False) *Cassie lives in an apartment.* **2.** Cassie's place has two bedrooms and one bathroom. (True) False **3.** Cassie's apartment has a large kitchen and a small living room. True (False) *Cassie's apartment has a small kitchen and a large living room.* **4.** Tom lives in a house. (True) False **5.** Tom's place has three bedrooms and two bathrooms. True (False) *Tom's house has four bedrooms and two bathrooms.* **6.** Tom's place doesn't have a yard. True (False) *Tom has a yard.*

PRACTICE 1

Read and listen to the audio script. Look at the answer key. Underline the answers in the audio script. 3.10

Audio Script	Answer Key
Mistakes are bad, right? Not always! Believe it or not, many inventions were actually mistakes at first. The potato chip was created by mistake at a restaurant in New York. One of the customers at the restaurant didn't want to eat the chef's French fries. The customer complained that they were too thick. After trying many times to please the customer, the chef got mad and sliced the potatoes really thin and fried them. The customer and everyone else loved them. That is how the potato chip was invented!	**1.** Are mistakes always bad? Answer: **No** **2.** Where was the potato chip created? Answer: **New York** **3.** Why didn't the customer want to eat the chef's French fries? Answer: **The French fries were too thick.** **4.** What did the chef do after the customer complained? Answer: **He sliced the potatoes thinly and fried them.** **5.** Did the customer like them? Answer: **Yes, the customer loved them.**

PRACTICE 2

Read and listen to the audio script. Look at the answer key. Underline the answers in the audio script. 3.11

Audio Script	Answer Key
Mathew: Hi, Allison. Allison: Hi, Matthew. Matthew: Do you want to get together on Saturday? Allison: Yes. What do you want to do? Matthew: Do you want to go to a football match? Allison: I don't like football. It's boring. How about shopping? Matthew: No, I don't want to go shopping. I went shopping last weekend. Allison: How about going to the cinema? Matthew: Yes, let's go to the cinema. Allison: What do you want to see? Matthew: Let's see an action film. Allison: Sounds good!	**1.** Does Allison want to get together with Matthew on Saturday? Answer: **Yes, she does.** **2.** Why doesn't Allison like football? Answer: **It's boring.** **3.** Why doesn't Matthew want to go shopping? Answer: **He went shopping last weekend.** **4.** Does Matthew want to go to the cinema? Answer: **Yes, he does.** **5.** What type of film does Matthew want to see? Answer: **He wants to see an action film.**

REFLECT

How confident are you with these tasks? Write each task in one of the columns: *Confident*, *Somewhat Confident*, or *Not Confident*.

answer the questions in the student book	find the answers in the audio script
mark the answers in the audio script	read the audio script
read the answer key	understand the audio recording

Confident	Somewhat Confident	Not Confident

LESSON 3 UNDERSTANDING READING TEXTS IN STUDENT MATERIALS

PREVIEW

You can preview reading texts in student materials. This helps you prepare for the lesson.

In Lesson 3, you will:

- read different types of student texts.
- find answers to questions in student texts.
- search for specific information in student materials.

Language to Know

answer key	blog	definition	paragraph	website
article	chart	letter	passage	

What Do You Know?

How often do your students do these reading activities? Write each activity in one of the columns: *Often*, *Sometimes*, or *Rarely*.

find words in a paragraph	read a chart	read a passage	read the question
match words to definitions	read a conversation	read a story	read the sentence
match words to pictures	read a letter	read a website	
read a blog	read an article		

Often	Sometimes	Rarely

LEARN 1

Read the conversation. Look at the answer key. Notice the highlighted answers in the conversation.

READING PASSAGE	ANSWER KEY
Faye: Hi, Alex. How do you like your new secondary school? Alex: I like it a lot. Faye: Have you got a uniform? Alex: Yes, I do. I have to wear blue trousers and a white shirt. Faye: Does your school have a canteen? Alex: Yes, it does. We can buy lunch there or bring your own. Faye: What do you usually do? Alex: I usually bring my own lunch. Faye: Do you ever buy lunch? Alex: Yes, I buy lunch on pizza day!	**1.** Does Alex like his new school? Answer: **Yes** **2.** What does Alex wear to school? Answer: **A uniform (blue trousers and a white shirt)** **3.** Does Alex's school have a canteen? Answer: **Yes** **4.** What does Alex usually do for lunch? Answer: **He brings his own lunch.** **5.** When does Alex buy lunch? Answer: **On pizza day**

LEARN 2

Read the passage. Look at the answer key. Notice the highlighted answers in the passage.

READING PASSAGE	ANSWER KEY
Penguins Penguins are a type of bird. They are different from other birds because they cannot fly. Penguins spend much of their time under water, and they are excellent swimmers. Penguins eat fish and other sea life. There are eighteen different kinds of penguins in the world. The Fairy Penguin is the smallest and weighs only two pounds. The Emperor Penguin is the largest. It can weigh up to ninety pounds.	**1.** Penguins can fly. True (False) **2.** Most penguins cannot swim well. True (False) **3.** Penguins eat fish and other sea life. (True) False **4.** There are sixteen kinds of penguins in the world. True (False) **5.** The Emperor Penguin is the largest penguin. (True) False

PRACTICE 1

Read the letter. Look at the answer key. Underline the answers in the letter.

LETTER	ANSWER KEY
Dear Linda, How are you? I'm fine. Friday was my last day of school. I am on holiday now. I am going to go swimming all summer long! My family is also going to go on a trip. We are going camping. This will be my first time sleeping in a tent. I am very excited. I miss you very much. Please come visit me soon. Maybe you can come camping with us! Sincerely, Susie	**1.** Friday was Susie's last day of ________. a. camp (b.) school c. holiday **2.** Susie is going to go ________ all summer long. a. camping b. visiting (c.) swimming **3.** Susie's family is going to go on a ________. (a.) trip b. ride c. hike **4.** It will be Susie's first time sleeping in a ________. a. park (b.) tent c. school **5.** Susie asks Linda to ________. a. go to school b. go on holiday (c.) visit soon

PRACTICE 2

Read the passage. Look at the answer key. Underline the answers in the passage.

READING PASSAGE	ANSWER KEY
I am lucky because I have two pets. I have a bird and a cat. My bird's name is Charlie. He is small and has long feathers. He has lots of energy. I play with him in my room. We have fun together. He is a good friend. My cat's name is Tabby. She is big and has short fur. She sleeps on a blanket. She likes to stay warm. Sometimes she plays in my room. She is a good friend. I love both of my pets.	**1.** Sam has three pets. True (False) **2.** Sam's bird is small and has short feathers. True (False) **3.** Sam plays with Charlie in his room. (True) False **4.** Tabby is small and has long fur. True (False) **5.** Tabby sleeps on a blanket. (True) False

REFLECT

How confident are you with these tasks? Write each task in one of the columns: *Confident*, *Somewhat Confident*, or *Not Confident*.

answer the questions in the student book	look at the answer key	read the text
find the answers in the text	mark the answers in the text	

Confident	Somewhat Confident	Not Confident

LESSON 4 WRITING CONTENT FROM STUDENT MATERIALS

PREVIEW

You can use your class textbook to give examples and highlight key information.

In Lesson 4, you will:
- find useful examples in student materials.
- copy examples from student materials.
- write examples on the board.
- use student materials to make worksheets.

Language to Know

explanation	phrase	vocabulary
instruction	textbook	worksheet

What Do You Know?

Do these words appear in your student materials? Write each word in one of the columns: *Words in My Student Materials* or *Words Not in My Student Materials*.

conversations	examples	goals	phrases	vocabulary
definitions	explanations	instructions	questions	

Words in My Student Materials	Words Not in My Student Materials

LEARN 1

A teacher prepared a grammar lesson on past continuous verbs. Look at the writing example sentences the teacher wrote on the board. Notice the highlighted sentences in the passages.

READING PASSAGE	EXAMPLE SENTENCE
1. The most exciting thing about my trip to the beach was the day I saw a shark! I was at the beach with my family. I was very hot, so I went in the water. I was swimming when a man yelled, "Shark!" So I got out of the water very fast!	I was swimming when a man yelled, "Shark!"
2. My brother and I were visiting our grandparents. They have a cat named Whiskers. One day my brother opened the back door and Whiskers ran out. We looked for her all afternoon. She didn't come home for three days! We were so worried.	My brother and I were visiting our grandparents.
3. The last time I was at the airport I went to get my bag. I was waiting for my bag when I saw someone take it! I said, "Excuse me!" The man turned and asked me what was wrong. He showed me the bag. It was not really mine. My bag came out a couple of minutes later. I was very embarrassed.	I was waiting for my bag when I saw someone take it!
4. Last Sunday, I went for a walk. It was sunny and warm, so I didn't bring an umbrella or raincoat. I walked to the big hill near my house. Then the sky got very dark. While I was walking up the hill, it started to rain very hard. I got really wet.	While I was walking up the hill, it started to rain very hard.

LEARN 2

A teacher prepared a cloze activity from a reading passage. Read the passage. Notice the highlighted sentences in the passage.

READING PASSAGE	CLOZE ACTIVITY
Dear Diary, Monday, June 17 Today I took the bus to the city. First, I got two books at the library. Then I went to the bank to get some money for lunch. I ate a sandwich at my favorite café. After that, I walked to the post office to send a letter. Finally, I went to the bus stop to go home. The bus came, and I looked for my wallet, but it was gone! I went back to the post office to find it, but it wasn't there. I ran to the police station and found my wallet. A kind person gave my wallet to the police. I was lucky. What a happy ending!	**1.** First, I got two books at the ________. **2.** Then I went to the ________ to get some money for lunch. **3.** I ate a sandwich at my favorite ________. **4.** After that, I walked to the ________ to send a letter. **5.** Finally, I went to the ________ to go home. **6.** I ran to the ________ and found my wallet.

PRACTICE 1

You are preparing a vocabulary lesson. Look at the vocabulary chart. Then underline the vocabulary in the conversation. There are 12 words in the conversation.

Colors		Clothing	
black	pink	baseball cap	dress
blue	red	hat	jacket
green	white	shirt	sweater
orange	yellow		

Kim: Hey, Paul. Is that your camera?

Paul: Yeah. I got it for my birthday. Do you want to see some pictures of my family?

Kim: Sure.

Paul: Here's one of us at my birthday party. That's my sister in the green shirt, and that's my brother next to her.

Kim: I see him. He's the one with the white baseball cap and the red jacket. Who's this wearing the orange hat?

Paul: That's my cousin, Steve. And behind him, in the yellow dress, that's my aunt, Marta.

Kim: Where are you?

Paul: It's hard to see me. I'm in the back, wearing a blue sweater.

PRACTICE 2

You are preparing a grammar lesson on count and noncount nouns. Read the text. Write the bold-faced nouns in the correct columns.

1. Hi Amanda,

How are you? Can you come to my party on Saturday? A lot of **friends** from school are coming. There will be a lot of great **food**. We're making **burgers**. And my mom is baking **bread** and her special **cookies**. I hope you can come. Let me know!

Nicholas

Count Nouns	Noncount Nouns
______________________	______________________
______________________	______________________

2. Hi Nicholas,

Of course, I can come! I just have to finish my homework first. What should I bring? Would you like me to make some **pasta**? Or maybe I can bring some **drinks**. How about some **juice**? I could bring a couple of **bottles**. I can't wait. See you there!

Amanda

Count Nouns	Noncount Nouns
____________________	____________________
____________________	____________________

REFLECT

What will you write from student textbooks to give examples or make activities? Write each item in one of the columns: *Will Write* or *Will Not Write.*

conversations	example	goals	paragraphs	questions
definitions	explanations	instructions	phrases	vocabulary

Will Write	Will Not Write

LESSON 5 REVIEW

1 Read the activity instructions. Then choose *True* or *False*.

Activity Instructions: Match the vocabulary with the definitions.

1. **Students should match words with meanings.**
   a. True
   b. False

Activity Instructions: Work in a group. Answer the questions.

2. **Students should work in pairs to answer the questions.**
   a. True
   b. False

Activity Instructions: Practice the conversation. Ask your partner about his or her family.

3. **Students should ask partners about their friends.**
   a. True
   b. False

Activity Instructions: Choose one of the following activities. Use the chart to answer the questions.

4. **Students only do one activity.**
   a. True
   b. False

Activity Instructions: Fill in the blanks using the new vocabulary. Underline the verbs in the sentence. Then check your answers with a partner.

5. **Students should fill in the blanks with the verbs.**
   a. True
   b. False

2 Read and listen to the audio script. Write the answers to the questions. Underline the answers in the audio script. 3.12

Audio Script	Questions
I am John, and I love to climb! When I was young, my mother told me that I climbed to the roof of my house! I am now a rock climber. I use big, strong ropes to hold me as I climb the side of a mountain. My friend holds the rope for me on the ground. When I get to the top of the mountain, I rappel down. Rappel means to go down. It is a lot of fun, and the view from the top is beautiful!	**1.** What does John love to do? ______ **2.** Where did John climb when he was young? ______ **3.** What does John use to hold him as he climbs the side of the mountain? ______ **4.** What does his friend do? ______ **5.** What does "rappel" mean? ______

3 Read the letter. Then choose the sentence that answers the question.

Letter	Questions
Dear Aunt Sally, (1) I'm having a great time in England. (2) We saw the sights in London yesterday. (3) I liked the castles and churches. (4) Today we went to Stonehenge. (5) It's a mystery! (6) It was built thousands of years ago and nobody knows how! (7) Tomorrow we go to Oxford to see one of the oldest universities. (8) I'm excited to go, and I might even go punting down the river, too. (9) Punting is when you sit in a boat and use a pole to make the boat go. (10) I wish you were here!	**1.** Which country is Tommy in? a. Sentence 1 b. Sentence 2 c. Sentence 3 d. Sentence 4 **2.** What did Tommy like about London? a. Sentence 2 b. Sentence 3 c. Sentence 5 d. Sentence 7 **3.** When was Stonehenge built? a. Sentence 4 b. Sentence 5 c. Sentence 6 d. Sentence 7 **4.** Where is one of the oldest universities? a. Sentence 5 b. Sentence 7 c. Sentence 8 d. Sentence 9 **5.** What is "punting"? a. Sentence 7 b. Sentence 8 c. Sentence 9 d. Sentence 10

4 **Read the prepositions in the chart. Then find these prepositions in the conversation and underline them. There are seven prepositions in the conversation, and some appear twice.**

Prepositions of Location	
behind	on the left
between	on the right
in front of	

Conversation: Where is the library?

Visitor: Excuse me. Can you tell me where the library is?

Student: Yes. It's between the music room and the office.

Visitor: Is it on the left side of the hallway?

Student: No, it's not on the left. It's on the right.

Visitor: So the library is behind the office?

Student: Oh, no; it's not behind it. It's in front of it.

Visitor: OK. I see the music room first then I see the library. I understand!

5 **Read the grammar information and the reading passage. Write the adverbs from the passage.**

Adverbs

Form: Adjective + *-ly*
Example: *They talked quietly.*

Reading Passage

Last night I walked in the woods. The moon was big and full. An owl hooted. I could hear it clearly. I walked slowly on my way. Then a bat flew silently by! I ran out of the woods quickly, looking carefully all around until I got home!

1. ______________________

2. ______________________

3. ______________________

4. ______________________

5. ______________________

UNIT 4 RESEARCH BRIEF
COMMUNICATING LESSON CONTENT: Engaging Students

The language and routines in Unit 4 help you to communicate the content of your lesson and engage your students. Here is some research supporting this unit.

What does student engagement mean?

Student engagement is how much students are interested, curious, and excited during a lesson. It also shows how much students participate in a lesson. Their engagement is often connected with their level of motivation. Student engagement also includes the amount of effort students make to learn the content. If students have negative attitudes about the content, the classroom environment, and/or the school, they may be less involved in the learning activities. Student engagement can take different forms. For example, students can be engaged in discussions, listening, reading, or writing. In each of these forms of engagement, the student actively participates.

Why does student engagement matter?

Teachers know that student engagement is essential for student learning. If students are not engaged, they are less likely to learn. For this reason, teachers use a variety of strategies to promote[1] student engagement. One instructional strategy may include stating clear lesson goals. Teachers may also scaffold[2] instruction by modeling a process or providing many examples to make content clear. Teachers may also encourage participation by asking students questions. These activities help to engage students with the lesson content.

A research study

HOW DO TEACHERS GRADUALLY RELEASE RESPONSIBILITY TO STUDENTS TO PROMOTE STUDENT ENGAGEMENT?

In 1983, Pearson and Gallagher reviewed years of research studies on reading instruction. Pearson and Gallagher then put their findings together. Their important review identified key traits[3] seen across the research studies. Based on these key traits, the authors created a model of instruction called the *Gradual Release of Responsibility.*

In this model, they identified four stages of instruction. First, the teacher models the strategy, and the students observe. During the second and third phases, the teacher and the students co-model the strategy. In the final stage, the teacher gives the students responsibility, and the students independently perform the strategy. Other researchers have confirmed[4] the effectiveness of this model. In 2010, Archer and Hughes called this model the *I do*, *We do*, *You do* model. Whether teachers call it the *Gradual Release of Responsibility* or *I do, We do, You do*, the process provides support as students engage with content.

[1] promote: to support
[2] scaffold: to support
[3] trait: characteristic, feature
[4] confirm: to prove, say that something is correct

Research questions and findings

Below are some questions researchers have asked about how to engage students. Findings of these studies are listed after each question.

1. **How do teachers begin to engage students with the content?**
   Teachers

   a. communicate clear lesson goals (Beesley & Apthorp, 2010; Seidel, Rimmele, & Prenzel, 2005).

   b. activate[5] students' prior[6] knowledge (Forrokhi & Modarres, 2012; Seidel et al., 2005).

   c. provide direct, clear instruction for content or vocabulary terms (Brosh, 1996; Frey & Fisher, 2010; Sonbul & Schmitt, 2009).

   d. emphasize[7] key concepts through repetition (Anderman, Andrzejewski, & Allen, 2011).

2. **How do teachers ensure content is clear for students?**
   Teachers

   a. model content, strategy, or language (Archer & Hughes, 2010; Frey & Fisher, 2010; Pearson & Gallagher, 1983).

   b. ask students to participate in the modeling process and confirm that students understand (Archer & Hughes, 2010; Frey & Fisher, 2010; Pearson & Gallagher, 1983).

   c. break instruction into small steps (Beesley & Apthorp, 2010; Frey & Fisher, 2010).

   d. ask different types of questions (Frey & Fisher, 2010).

3. **How do teachers communicate expectations to promote student engagement?**
   Teachers

   a. tell students what is on assessments (Anderman et al., 2011).

   b. provide clear instructions for activities (Marzano & Pickering, 2003).

   c. ask questions to help make instructions clear (Frey & Fisher, 2010).

[5] activate: to start
[6] prior: from before
[7] emphasize: to stress, focus on

UNIT 4 COMMUNICATING LESSON CONTENT

LESSON 1 UNDERSTANDING AND COMMUNICATING LESSON GOALS

PREVIEW

You can communicate lesson goals in English.

In Lesson 1, you will:
- review lesson goals from previous classes.
- sequence lesson goals.
- summarize lesson goals.
- respond to student comments.

Language to Know

communicate	furniture	review	sequence
finally	previous	room	summarize

What Do You Know?

Write the phrases you know for communicating lesson goals in English. Examples are below:

Reviewing from the Previous Class	Sequencing Lesson Goals	Summarizing the Lesson
What did we do yesterday?	*First, we are going to...*	*What did we learn today?*

Rate your confidence using these phrases. Put a check below your confidence level.

not confident	a little confident	somewhat confident	very confident

LEARN 1

A. Here are some phrases for reviewing from the previous class. Listen and repeat. 4.1

Reviewing from the Previous Class

Let's review yesterday's lesson.

What did we do yesterday?

Who can tell me what we talked about yesterday?

Who remembers what we talked about last class?

Are there any questions?

B. There are many substitutions for these phrases. Listen and repeat. 4.2

Phrases	Substitutions
Let's review yesterday's lesson.	Let's review these words. Let's review today's lesson. Let's review what you learned.
What did we do yesterday?	What did we learn yesterday?
Who can tell me what we talked about yesterday?	Who can tell me what we did yesterday? Who can tell me what we learned yesterday? Who can tell me what we studied yesterday?
Who remembers what we talked about last class?	Who remembers what we did last class? Who remembers what we studied last class? Who remembers what we learned last class?
Are there any questions?	Are there any questions about the vocabulary? Are there any questions about the past tense? Are there any questions about the reading?

LEARN 2

Read the conversation, and watch the video. Listen to the teacher review the previous day's lesson. ▶ 4.1

Mrs. Chen: Good morning class. Let's review yesterday's lesson. Who can tell me what we studied yesterday?

Lin Fang: Rooms in a house.

Mrs. Chen: Yes. Let's look at that vocabulary again. Please name the room where food is prepared.

Wang Bo: The kitchen.

Mrs. Chen: Good. And, the room where you sleep?

Lin Fang: The bedroom.

Mrs. Chen: Good! Today, we will continue this lesson. First, are there any questions?

Wang Bo: Yes, I have a question about the word "living room."

Mrs. Chen: Yes?

Wang Bo: Is it one word or two?

Mrs. Chen: It is two words.

LEARN 3

A. Here are some phrases for sequencing lesson goals. Listen and repeat. 4.3

Sequencing Lesson Goals

Today, we're going to continue our unit.

Today, we will continue learning words for rooms in a house.

In this unit, you are going to study words about the house.

In this lesson, you're going to work on talking about houses.

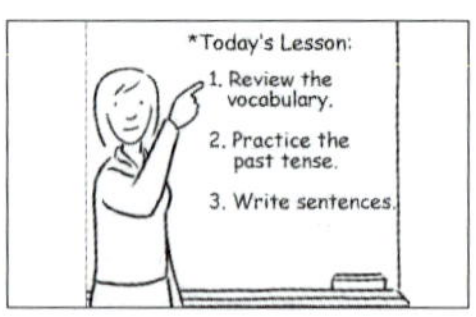

First, we are going to review the vocabulary.

Then, we are going to practice the past tense.

Finally, we will write sentences.

B. There are many substitutions for these phrases. Listen and repeat. 4.4

Phrases	Substitutions
Today, we're going to continue our unit.	Today, we're going to do a project. Today, we're going to practice the new words. Today, we're going to learn how to say likes and dislikes.
Today, we will continue learning words for rooms in a house.	Today, we will read a story. Today, we will play a game. Today, we will write a story. Today, we will start a new unit.
In this unit, you are going to study words about the house.	In this unit, you are going to practice the past tense. In this unit, you are going to learn how to ask for help.
In this lesson, you're going to work on talking about houses.	In this lesson, you're going to look at the present tense.
First, we are going to review the vocabulary.	First, we are going to do an activity.
Then, we are going to practice the past tense.	Then, we are going to look at the homework.
Finally, we will write sentences.	Finally, we will read a story.

LEARN 4

Read the teacher's notes on the board. Listen to the teacher talk about the order of the lesson. 4.5

Today we will... 1. Review rooms in a house 2. Learn words for furniture 3. Read a story 4. Play a game	**Mrs. Chen:** OK, class. Today, we're going to continue our unit on houses. In this lesson, you are going to learn words for furniture. First, we will review the rooms in a house. Then, we are going to learn words for furniture. Next, we are going to read a story about Tommy's house. Finally, we are going to play a game to practice all of the new words. Are there any questions?

LEARN 5

A. Here are some phrases for summarizing the day's lesson. Listen and repeat. 4.6

Summarizing the Day's Lesson

What did we learn today?

I want to go over what we learned today.

Let's review what we learned today.

Today, we talked about words for rooms.

Let's look at that vocabulary again.

B. There are many substitutions for these phrases. Listen and repeat. 4.7

Phrases	Substitutions
Today, we talked about words for rooms.	Today, we learned new words. Today, we reviewed the past tense. Today, we worked on ordering food.
Let's look at that vocabulary again.	Let's look at the past tense again. Let's look at making introductions again.

LEARN 6

Read the teacher's question on the board. Listen to the teacher summarize the lesson. 4.8

What did we learn today?	**Mrs. Chen:** OK, class. Let's review what we learned today about furniture. What is in a living room? **Wang Bo:** A couch. **Mrs. Chen:** Good. What else? **Lin Fang:** Tables. **Wang Bo:** Can you give another example? **Mrs. Chen:** A chair. **Wang Bo:** I don't understand. **Mrs. Chen:** A chair is a type of furniture. You are sitting on a chair. Let's look at that vocabulary again.

PRACTICE 1

Write the sentences in the correct columns.

Finally, we are going to write sentences.	Then, we're going to listen to a story.
I want to go over what we learned today.	Today, we talked about things in a house.
In this unit, you are going to study words about the family.	Today, we're going to practice a conversation.
Let's review what we learned today.	What did we learn yesterday?
Next, you will play a game.	Who remembers what we talked about last class?

Reviewing/Summarizing	Communicating Goals/Sequencing

PRACTICE 2

Choose the correct answer.

1. **_______________ did we do yesterday?**
   a. When
   b. What
   c. Why
   d. Where

2. **_______________ review what we learned today.**
   a. We
   b. Let's
   c. Can
   d. You

3. **_______________ did we learn today?**
   a. What
   b. Why
   c. Who
   d. How

4. **Who _______________ what we did yesterday?**
   a. forgets
   b. tells
   c. speaks
   d. remembers

5. **Are there _______________ questions?**
   a. few
   b. none
   c. any
   d. your

6. **Who can tell me what we talked _______________ yesterday?**
   a. on
   b. about
   c. in
   d. at

7. **Let's _______________ that vocabulary again.**
   a. look at
   b. continue
   c. begin
   d. talk

8. **Today we worked _______________ words for rooms in a house.**
   a. on
   b. about
   c. in
   d. the

9. **I want to go _______________ what we learned today.**
   a. in
   b. on
   c. over
   d. there

10. **Who remembers _______________ we studied last class?**
    a. that
    b. about
    c. what
    d. which

PRACTICE 3

Write instructions to your students to communicate the lesson goal. One example is below:

Lesson Goal	Sentence
practice greetings	*In this lesson, you are going to practice greetings.*

	Lesson Goals	Sentences
1.	learn adjectives	
2.	review vocabulary	
3.	start a project	
4.	review the past tense	
5.	a. read the story b. answer questions	
6.	a. listen to a conversation b. practice the conversation	
7.	a. listen to a conversation b. write a conversation c. practice conversation with partner	
8.	a. look at the future tense b. review the future tense c. write sentences with future tense	
9.	a. read about food around the world b. talk about your favorite food c. write about your favorite food d. begin a project on food	

REFLECT

Think about what you learned in this lesson. Write five phrases you practiced.

Phrases for Understanding and Communicating Lesson Goals

Now rate your confidence using these phrases. Put a check below your confidence level.

not confident	a little confident	somewhat confident	very confident

LESSON 2 ENGAGING STUDENTS IN THE TOPIC

PREVIEW

You can ask students questions about the lesson topic in English. This helps get students interested in the lesson.

In Lesson 2, you will:

- ask questions to engage your students in the topic.
- help students to think about the topic.
- get students to talk about the topic.

Language to Know

animal	cow	farm	horse	panda bear
chicken	engage	giraffe	lion	zoo

What Do You Know?

Write the phrases you know for engaging your students in a topic in English.

What do you know about...?

LEARN 1

A. Here are some phrases for engaging students in the topic. Listen and repeat. 4.9

Engaging Students in the Topic

Think about animals in a zoo.

What do you know about zoo animals?

Look at the picture. What do you see?

What words do you know?

Can you tell me other animals?

Have you ever seen a lion?

Did you ever see a panda bear?

Were you ever on a farm?

B. There are many substitutions for these phrases. Listen and repeat. 4.10

Phrases	Substitutions
Think about animals in a zoo.	Think about animals in Africa. Think about your favorite animals.
What do you know about zoo animals?	What do you know about panda bears?
What words do you know?	What animals do you know?
Can you tell me other animals?	Can you tell me about the zoo? Can you tell me where they live?
Have you ever seen a lion?	Have you ever gone to a zoo? Have you ever been to Africa?
Did you ever see a panda bear?	Did you ever go to a farm?

LEARN 2

Read the conversation, and watch the video. Listen to the teacher engage students in the topic. ▶ 4.2

Mrs. Chen: Today, we're going to talk about animals in a zoo. Look at the picture. What do you see?
Lin Fang: A panda.
Mrs. Chen: Yes. Have you ever seen a panda bear?
Lin Fang: Yes, in a zoo.
Mrs. Chen: Great. Can you tell me other animals in a zoo? Wang Bo?
Wang Bo: Lions.
Mrs. Chen: Yes. There are lions in a zoo. Think about other animals in a zoo. Look at the pictures. What words do you know?
Lin Fang: Elephant.
Mrs. Chen: Yes! There are elephants in a zoo. Did you ever see this animal in a zoo?
Wang Bo: Yes, but I don't know the word.
Mrs. Chen: It's a giraffe.

PRACTICE 1

Choose the correct answer.

1. **__________ words do you know?**
   a. What
   b. When
   c. Where
   d. How

2. **__________ do you know about panda bears?**
   a. What
   b. When
   c. Where
   d. Who

3. **Have you __________ been to Africa?**
   a. never
   b. ever
   c. go
   d. gone

4. **__________ you ever on a farm?**
   a. Do
   b. Have
   c. Did
   d. Were

5. **__________ you tell me about zoos?**
   a. What
   b. How
   c. Can
   d. Do

6. **__________ you ever see a panda bear?**
   a. What
   b. Did
   c. Where
   d. When

7. **Can you __________ me other animals?**
   a. think
   b. tell
   c. talk
   d. know

8. **What __________ you see?**
   a. done
   b. have
   c. were
   d. do

9. **Look ______________ the picture.**
   a. at
   b. to
   c. with
   d. about

10. **Think ______________ animals in a zoo.**
   a. about
   b. on
   c. in
   d. around

PRACTICE 2

Fill in the blanks with the phrases.

animals do you know	Did you ever	do you see	Think about	you ever on a farm
at the picture	do you know about	Look at	you ever been on a horse	you tell me other animals

Teacher: Look ______________________________. What ______________________________?
Student: A farm.

Teacher: Were ______________________________?
Student: Yes.

Teacher: What farm ______________________________?
Student: Cow.

Teacher: Good. Can ______________________________?
Student: Horse.

Teacher: Yes. Have ______________________________?
Student: No.

Teacher: ______________________________ other animals on a farm.
______________________________ the picture again.
Student: Chickens.

Teacher: What ______________________________ chickens?
Student: They lay eggs.

Teacher: Good. ______________________________ eat an egg?
Student: Yes. They are good.

REFLECT

Think about what you learned in this lesson. Write five phrases you practiced.

Phrases for Engaging Students in the Topic

Now rate your confidence using these phrases. Put a check below your confidence level.

not confident	a little confident	somewhat confident	very confident

LESSON 3 EXPLAINING LESSON CONTENT

PREVIEW

You can explain lesson content to your students in English.

In Lesson 3, you will:

- explain lesson content.
- write explanations of lesson content.

Language to Know

fork	knife	seed	stem	vegetable
future	past	spoon	utensil	

What Do You Know?

Write the phrases you know for explaining lesson content. One example is below:

We use "will" to talk about the future.

LEARN 1

A. Here are some phrases for explaining lesson content. Listen and repeat. 4.11

Explaining Lesson Content

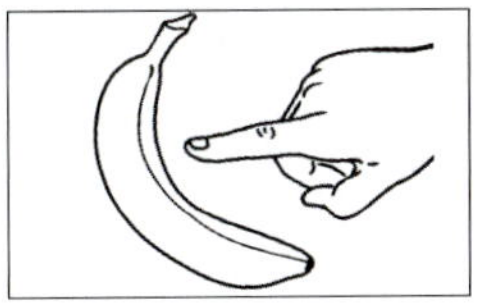

This is a banana.

That is an apple.

A banana is a fruit.

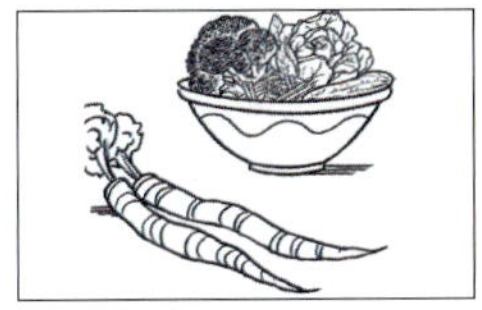

Carrots are vegetables.

It is a fruit.

It has seeds.

They are forks.

This means small.

B. There are many substitutions for these phrases. Listen and repeat. 4.12

Phrases	Substitutions
This is a banana.	This is an orange.
That is an apple.	That is a table.
It is a fruit.	It is red. It is big.
It has seeds.	It has a stem.
They are forks.	They are spoons.
This means small.	This means very good.

LEARN 2

Read the conversation, and watch the video. Listen to the teacher explain lesson content. 4.3

Mrs. Chen: Today, we're going to learn some words for food and eating. Let's turn to page 46. What is this?

Lin Fang: Carrot.

Mrs. Chen: Yes. This is a carrot. It is a vegetable. What about that?

Wang Bo: Apple.

Mrs. Chen: That's right. That is an apple. An apple is a fruit. What else do you see?

Lin Fang: Spoon. Forks.

Mrs. Chen: Good. This is a spoon. They are forks. They are utensils. Utensils mean forks, spoons, and knives. When we want to eat, we use utensils.

LEARN 3

A. Here are some more phrases for explaining lesson content. Listen and repeat. 4.13

Explaining Lesson Content

This is how you end a sentence.

You use this to talk about the future.

We say "is sleeping" when we talk about what is happening now.

We use -ed after a verb when we talk about the past.

When we want to say, "You're welcome" we say, "Don't mention it."

B. There are many substitutions for these phrases. Listen and repeat. 4.14

Phrases	Substitutions
This is how you end a sentence.	This is how you write "utensils."
You use this to talk about the future.	You use a period to end a sentence. You use an *-s* after nouns to mean more than one.
We say "is sleeping" when we talk about what is happening now.	We say "excellent" when something is very good.
We use *-ed* after a verb when we talk about the past.	We use "in" after "sleep" to mean "sleep late." We use *-ing* after a verb when we talk about something that is happening right now.
When we want to say, "You're welcome" we say, "Don't mention it."	When we want to talk about tomorrow, we use the future.

LEARN 4

Read the conversation as you listen to the teacher explain the lesson content. 4.15

Mrs. Chen: Look at the picture on page 92. What is happening? Wang Bo?

Wang Bo: Boys swimming.

Mrs. Chen: The boys are swimming. In this sentence, we use the word "are" when we have a verb that ends in *-ing*. What is the girl doing? Lin Fang?

Lin Fang: She is eat.

Mrs. Chen: Try adding *-ing*. We use *-ing* after a verb when we talk about something that is happening right now.

Lin Fang: She is eating.

Mrs. Chen: Good job, Lin Fang! What is the boy by the tree doing? Wang Bo?

Wang Bo: He is reading.

Mrs. Chen: That's right. When we want to say that it is happening right now, we say, "He is reading."

PRACTICE 1

Fill in the blanks with the words and phrases.

a banana	apple	are fruits	want to say, "You're welcome"
has seeds	say, "Don't mention it"	when we talk about the past	use a knife to cut food
forks	something is very good	you write "apple"	

1. This is ______________________________.
2. They are ______________________________.
3. It ______________________________.
4. That is an ______________________________.
5. Apples ______________________________.
6. This is how ______________________________.
7. You ______________________________.
8. When we ______________________________ we ______________________________.
9. We use *-ed* after a verb ______________________________.
10. We say "excellent" when ______________________________.

PRACTICE 2

Fill in the blanks with the phrases.

A banana is a	It has	That is a banana	This is how you	This means
we use	We use "will" before	We use "will" with a verb	When we want to	You use an

Teacher: Are there any questions?
Student A: What is "will"?

Teacher: ________________ to talk about the future.
Student A: How do we use it?

Teacher: ________________ a verb. For example, "I will study." ________________ that I am going to do it in the future, not now. Are there any other questions?
Student B: What is this?

Teacher: ________________. ________________ fruit. ________________ a yellow peel. How many bananas do you see in this picture?
Student B: There are two banana.

Teacher: ________________ *-s* after nouns to make the word plural. Anything else?
Student C: Why does this have *-ed* at the end?

Teacher: ________________ talk about something in the past, ________________ *-ed*. ________________ form the past tense.

REFLECT

Think about what you learned in this lesson. Write five phrases you practiced.

Phrases for Explaining Lesson Content

Now rate your confidence using these phrases. Put a check below your confidence level.

not confident	a little confident	somewhat confident	very confident

LESSON 4 MODELING AND GIVING EXAMPLES

PREVIEW

You can model and give examples to your students in English. This will help students understand the lesson better.

In Lesson 4, you will:
- tell students to follow examples.
- encourage students to model for their classmates.
- create examples to guide student learning.
- respond to student questions on examples.

Language to Know

dialog	location	model	occupation	preposition

What Do You Know?

Write the phrases you know for modeling and giving examples. One example is below:

Here is an example of a preposition.

Rate your confidence using these phrases. Put a check below your confidence level.

not confident	a little confident	somewhat confident	very confident

LEARN 1

A. Here are some phrases for modeling and giving examples. Listen and repeat. 4.16

Modeling and Giving Examples

Please repeat after me.

Please read the sentences.

Please listen to the example.

Here's an example.

Here is an example of a preposition.

Let me give you an example of a preposition.

Look at these examples on the board.

Jack, please read the example.

Let's watch Anne and Jack.

B. There are many substitutions for these phrases. Listen and repeat. 4.17

Phrases	Substitutions
Please read the sentences.	Please read the words/dialog/examples/ conversation.
Please listen to the example.	Please listen to the example of the past tense. Please listen to the examples of prepositions.
Here is an example of a preposition.	Here is an example of an occupation. Here is an example of how to say "goodbye."
Look at these examples on the board.	Look at this example of a preposition.

LEARN 2

Read the conversation, and watch the video. Listen to the teacher model and give examples. ▶ 4.4

Mrs. Chen: Let's review yesterday's lesson on prepositions. Look at these examples of prepositions in the book. Turn to page 41. Lin Fang, please read the example.

Lin Fang: The girl is under the tree.

Mrs. Chen: Good. Class, please repeat the example after me. The girl is under the tree.

Class: The girl is under the tree.

Mrs. Chen: Excellent. Wang Bo, please read the next example of a preposition.

Wang Bo: The bird is above the tree.

Mrs. Chen: Yes. The bird is above the tree. Please repeat the sentence, class.

Class: The bird is above the tree.

Mrs. Chen: Let me give you another example. The basket is next to the girl. Let's watch Wang Bo and Lin Fang point to something that is next to them.

Wang Bo: Lin Fang is next to me.

Mrs. Chen: Good example!

PRACTICE 1

Choose the correct answer.

1. **Please ______________ after me.**
   a. see
   b. listen
   c. watch
   d. repeat

2. **______________ me give you an example.**
   a. Can
   b. Let
   c. Please
   d. Tell

3. **Here's ______________ example.**
   a. an
   b. a
   c. on
   d. in

4. **Look ______________ this example.**
   a. of
   b. to
   c. around
   d. at

5. **Please listen ______________ these examples.**
   a. on
   b. in
   c. to
   d. of

6. **Look at ______________ examples on page 45.**
   a. this
   b. that
   c. these
   d. about

7. **Please read the example ______________ a preposition.**
   a. of
   b. in
   c. to
   d. at

8. **Look at these examples ______________ the board.**
   a. down
   b. up
   c. on
   d. in

9. **Please repeat the sentence ______________ the recording.**
   a. at
   b. to
   c. of
   d. after

10. **______________ watch Anne and Jack.**
   a. Let
   b. Let's
   c. Here
   d. Here's

PRACTICE 2

Read the situation. Choose the correct answer. Then practice saying the answer aloud.

1. **You want students to repeat. You say:**
   a. Please repeat after me.
   b. Please read the conversation.
   c. Jack, please read the example.

2. **A student says, "Can you give an example?" You reply:**
   a. Please listen to the example.
   b. Here's an example.
   c. Let's watch Anne and Jack.

3. **You are going to read an example to students. You say:**
   a. Please repeat the examples.
   b. Please listen to the example.
   c. Please read the example.

4. **You are playing a recording for the class. You say:**
   a. Please repeat after me.
   b. Please repeat after the recording.
   c. Please read the dialog.

5. **You want the class to read examples you wrote. You say:**
   a. Jack, please read the example.
   b. Please listen to the example.
   c. Look at these examples on the board.

6. **You want one student to read the example. You say:**
   a. Jack, please read the example.
   b. Let's watch Anne and Jack.
   c. Please repeat after me.

7. **You want two students to model. You say:**
   a. Let me give you an example of a preposition.
   b. Please read the examples.
   c. Let's watch Anne and Jack.

8. **You want students to read from the text. You say:**
   a. Please read the sentences.
   b. Here's an example.
   c. Please listen to the dialog.

9. **You want to show your students a preposition. You say:**
   a. Here is an example of an occupation.
   b. Let me give you an example of a preposition.
   c. Please listen to the examples of prepositions.

10. **You want a student to give an example of a job. You say:**
   a. Jack, please read the example.
   b. Anne, please read the example of an occupation.
   c. Let me give you an example of an occupation.

PRACTICE 3

Read the example from the textbook. Write another example using the words.

1. Using "because"

	Example from textbook:	*Your example:*
Original:	I like swimming. It's fun.	reading/interesting
Combined:	I like swimming because it's fun.	______________________

2. Making Comparisons

	Example from textbook:	*Your example:*
Original:	Mary is tall. Tom is short.	John fast/Harry slow
Combined:	Mary is taller than Tom.	______________________

3. Using "but"

	Example from textbook:	*Your example:*
Original:	The book is difficult. The book is interesting.	movie/long/funny
Combined:	The book is difficult but interesting.	______________________

4. Asking Questions with "can"

	Example from textbook:	*Your example:*
Original:	She can ice skate.	baby/walk
Question:	Can she ice skate?	______________________

5. Making a noun plural

	Example from textbook:	*Your example:*
Original:	I have one book.	She/cat
Plural:	I have many books.	______________________

6. Using adjectives

	Example from textbook:	*Your example:*
Original:	I have a big bicycle. I have a red bicycle.	She/new/blue/pencil
Combined:	I have a big, red bicycle.	______________________

7. Using the superlative (*-est*)

	Example from textbook:	*Your example:*
Original:	She is a fast runner.	He/tall/boy
Superlative:	She is the fastest runner.	______________________

8. Using "always"

	Example from textbook:	*Your example:*
Original:	I watch a movie after school.	I/do/homework
Using "always":	I always watch a movie after school.	______________________

9. Using the possessive (-'s)

	Example from textbook:	*Your example:*
Original:	Tom has a pencil.	That/Mary/book
Possessive:	That is Tom's pencil.	______________________

10. Questions in the past tense

	Example from textbook:	*Your example:*
Original:	Bob went to school.	Jenny/ate/lunch
Past tense question:	Did Bob go to school?	______________________

REFLECT

Think about what you learned in this lesson. Write five phrases you practiced.

Phrases for Modeling and Giving Examples

Now rate your confidence using these phrases. Put a check below your confidence level.

not confident	a little confident	somewhat confident	very confident

LESSON 5 REVIEW A

1 Write the sentences in the correct columns.

Did you ever see a panda bear?
Finally, we are going to write sentences.
Please repeat after me.
Today we will practice writing a paragraph.
What words do you know?

Communicating Lesson Goals	Engaging Students in the Topic	Modeling and Giving Examples

2 Fill in the blanks with the words and phrases. Then practice the teacher's lines.

Can you tell me
Please repeat
look at the sentences
remembers
other phrases
we say

Teacher: Who ____________________ what we talked about last class?
Student: Asking for directions.

Teacher: Yes. ____________________ some sentences we learned?
Student: "Can you helping me?"

Teacher: ____________________ after me. "Can you help me?"
Student: "Can you help me?"

Teacher: Good! What ____________________ do you know?
Student: "Where is the post office?"

Teacher: Remember, when we want to ask for directions, ____________________ "excuse me" first. Now, ____________________ on page 45.

3 Choose the two correct responses for each question.

1. **Which phrases summarize the lesson?**
   a. Utensils means forks, spoons, and knives.
   b. Today we worked on ordering food.
   c. Let's look at the past tense again.
   d. Look at these examples on the board.

2. **Which phrases review from the previous lesson?**
   a. What do you know about zoo animals?
   b. Are there any questions about the article?
   c. First, we are going to do an activity.
   d. What did we learn yesterday?

3. **Which phrases engage students in the lesson?**
   a. Think about your favorite food.
   b. You use a dictionary to find words.
   c. Did you ever see a whale?
   d. That is how you end a sentence.

4. **Which phrases explain lesson content?**
   a. Please listen to the example.
   b. This is an apple.
   c. Carrots are vegetables.
   d. What words do you know?

5. **Which phrases are for modeling and giving examples?**
   a. Here's an example of a preposition.
   b. Look at the picture. What do you see?
   c. Let's watch Lin Fang and Wang Bo.
   d. First, we are going to do an activity.

4 Use the key words to write the teacher's questions and answers.

1. **Student:** Can you explain, please? — Key words: here/example
   Teacher: ____________________

2. **Teacher:** ____________________ — Key words: any/questions
   Student: No, I don't have any questions.

3. **Student:** This is a story about a horse. — Key words: ridden/horse
   Teacher: ____________________

4. **Student:** What will we do today? — Key words: today/practice/new words
   Teacher: ____________________

5. **Student:** Can you explain again? — Key words: when/want/say/"You're welcome"/"Don't mention it"
   Teacher: ____________________

LESSON 6 ASKING FOR AND WRITING STUDENT EXAMPLES

PREVIEW

You can ask students for examples in English.

In Lesson 6, you will:

- ask for student examples.
- write student examples.
- respond to student examples.

Language to Know

adjective	brush	cook	greeting	tooth
breakfast	compliment	furniture	routine	

What Do You Know?

Write the phrases you know for asking for and writing student examples. One example is below:

Give me an example of an animal.

Rate your confidence using these phrases. Put a check below your confidence level.

not confident	a little confident	somewhat confident	very confident

LEARN 1

A. Here are some phrases for asking for and writing student examples. Listen and repeat. 4.18

Asking for and Writing Student Examples

Give me an example of part of your morning routine.

Give me another example of an occupation.

Can you think of an example of a preposition?

Can you think of another example of a fruit?

Who can give an example of an adjective?

Who can give another example of an animal?

B. There are many substitutions for these phrases. Listen and repeat. 4.19

Phrases	Substitutions
Give me an example of part of your morning routine.	Give me an example of a greeting. Give me an example of the past tense.
Give me another example of an occupation.	Give me another example of a compliment. Give me another example of the future tense.
Can you think of an example of a preposition?	Can you think of an example of furniture? Can you think of an example of an animal?
Can you think of another example of a fruit?	Can you think of another example of a plural noun? Can you think of another example of a verb?
Who can give an example of an adjective?	Who can give an example of a zoo animal? Who can give an example of how to introduce yourself?
Who can give another example of an animal?	Who can give another example of a verb? Who can give another example of how to say "sorry"?

LEARN 2

Read the conversation, and watch the video. Listen to the teacher dismiss her class. ▶ 4.5

Mrs. Nowak: Today, we're going to talk about what you do in the morning. Who can give an example of part of your morning routine?
Julia: Eat breakfast.
Mrs. Nowak: Yes. We eat breakfast in the morning. Give me another example of part of your morning routine. Jakub?
Jakub: Brush teeth.
Mrs. Nowak: Great. Can you think of another example?
Julia: Go to school.
Mrs. Nowak: Yes, that's right. We all go to school in the morning.

PRACTICE 1

Choose the correct answer.

1. **Please ______________ me an example.**
   a. see
   b. listen
   c. take
   d. give

2. **______________ can tell me the answer?**
   a. Why
   b. When
   c. Who
   d. What

4. **Please give me ______________ example.**
   a. another
   b. other
   c. a
   d. some

6. **______________ you think of an example?**
   a. Please
   b. Why
   c. Can
   d. Does

5. **Please give an example ______________ an animal.**
   a. to
   b. of
   c. in
   d. at

3. **Please think ______________ an example of an animal.**
   a. on
   b. for
   c. in
   d. of

5. **Please give ______________ an example.**
   a. you
   b. to
   c. me
   d. at

7. **Please think of an ______________.**
   a. noun
   b. adjective
   c. verb
   d. word

PRACTICE 2

Read the situation. Choose the correct answer. Then practice saying the answer aloud.

1. **You want students to describe what they do in the morning. You say:**
   a. Give me an example of part of your morning routine.
   b. Give me an example of a greeting.
   c. Give me another example of an occupation.

2. **You want your students to name some prepositions. You say:**
   a. Can you think of an example of a preposition?
   b. Give me an example of a greeting.
   c. Who can give another example of a verb?

3. **You want students to describe a lion. You say:**
   a. Give me another example of a compliment.
   b. Who can give an example of an adjective?
   c. Give me an example of the past tense.

4. **You want your students to name different jobs. You say:**
   a. Can you think of another example of how to order food?
   b. Can you think of an example of a preposition?
   c. Give me another example of an occupation.

5. **A student says, "An apple is a fruit." You say:**
   a. Give me an example of a greeting.
   b. Can you think of another example of a fruit?
   c. Can you think of an example of furniture?

6. **A student says, "A giraffe is an animal." You say:**
   a. Who can give another example of an animal?
   b. Can you think of an example of how to order food?
   c. Give me an example of the past tense.

7. **You are teaching ways to say "hello." You say:**
   a. Who can give another example of how to say "sorry"?
   b. Can you think of an example of how to say "goodbye"?
   c. Give me an example of a greeting.

8. **You finished discussing singular nouns. Now you say:**
   a. Give me an example of the past tense.
   b. Can you think of an example of a plural noun?
   c. Who can give an example of an adjective?

9. **You are teaching ways to apologize. You say:**
   a. Can you think of an example of how to say "goodbye"?
   b. Give me an example of a greeting.
   c. Who can give another example of how to say "sorry"?

10. **You are teaching ways to say "farewell." You say:**
    a. Can you think of an example of how to say "goodbye"?
    b. Can you think of another example of how to order food?
    c. Who can give an example of how to introduce yourself?

REFLECT

Think about what you learned in this lesson. Write five phrases you practiced.

Phrases for Asking for and Writing Student Examples

Now rate your confidence using these phrases. Put a check below your confidence level.

not confident	a little confident	somewhat confident	very confident

LESSON 7 GIVING ACTIVITY INSTRUCTIONS A

PREVIEW

You can give students instructions in English before they begin activities. This gives students good listening practice.

In Lesson 7, you will:

- direct students to complete activities.
- explain activity instructions.
- write activity instructions clearly.
- respond to student questions on instructions.

Language to Know

alone	article	expression	partner	title
alternative	choose	guess	table	

What Do You Know?

Write the phrases you know for giving activity instructions in English. One example is below:

Practice the dialog.

Rate your confidence using these phrases. Put a check below your confidence level.

not confident	a little confident	somewhat confident	very confident

LEARN 1

A. Here are some phrases for giving activity instructions. Listen and repeat. 4.20

Giving Activity Instructions

Look at the picture.

Work with a partner.

Give information.

Play a game in pairs.

Think about your family.

Guess the word.

Take turns to read the paragraph.

Draw your ideas.

Circle the correct word.

Find a student.

Check your paper with a partner.

Choose a title for the article.

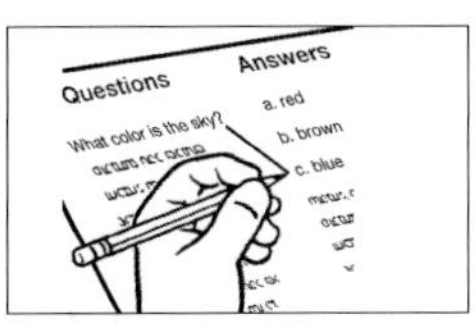

Match the questions and answers.

Practice saying the description.

Use your notes to write a paragraph.

B. There are many substitutions for these phrases. Listen and repeat. 4.21

Phrases	Substitutions
Look at the picture.	Look at the list. Look at the title. Look at the text. Look at the article. Look at page 20. Look at Exercise 5.
Work with a partner.	Work alone. Work in a group. Work in groups of three. Work in pairs. Work with a classmate.
Give information.	Give examples/instructions. Give each paragraph a title.
Play a game in pairs.	Play in teams. Play a guessing game. Play in groups of four.
Guess the word.	Guess the name/student/people.
Draw your ideas.	Draw a picture of your classroom.
Circle the correct word.	Circle the verb. Circle the alternative. Circle the photo.
Find a student.	Find a classmate/the answers/an example/the information.
Choose a title for the article.	Choose an object. Choose words from the table. Choose one of the following activities.
Match the questions and answers.	Match the sentences to the people. Match the expressions with the pictures.
Practice saying the description.	Practice giving the date. Practice reading the dialog. Practice introducing yourself.
Use your notes to write a paragraph.	Use the picture to write a paragraph. Use the words to write a paragraph. Use complete sentences to write a paragraph. Use the vocabulary in the text to write a paragraph. Use the information from the chart to write a paragraph.

LEARN 2

Read the conversation, and watch the video. Listen to a teacher give activity instructions. ▶ 4.6

Mrs. Nowak: OK, everyone, let's begin. Look at page 63.
Julia: What exercise number?
Mrs. Nowak: Exercise 3. Work with a partner. Take turns reading the paragraph. Then choose a title for the paragraph.
Jakub: How much time do we have?
Mrs. Nowak: You have 10 minutes.
Julia: Can you write the instructions, please?
Mrs. Nowak: Yes.
Jakub: We need more time, please, Mrs. Nowak.
Mrs. Nowak: You can have five more minutes. When you finish, use the information in the paragraph to answer these questions. Work alone to complete them.

PRACTICE 1

Choose the correct answer.

1. ______________ information.
a. Give
b. Work
c. Take
d. Play

2. ______________ the photo.
a. Work with
b. Look at
c. Practice
d. Write

3. ______________ the questions and answers.
a. Draw
b. Match
c. Use
d. Give

4. ______________ introducing yourself.
a. Practice
b. Draw
c. Talk
d. Work

5. Take ______________.
a. play
b. playing
c. turns
d. partners

6. Look ______________ the photo.
a. in
b. at
c. to
d. on

7. Think ______________ your family.
a. in
b. about
c. on
d. at

8. Play a game ______________ pairs.
a. with
b. at
c. in
d. for

9. Choose a title ______________ the article.
a. of
b. about
c. from
d. for

10. Use your ______________ to write a paragraph.
a. notes
b. complete sentences
c. exercise
d. classroom

PRACTICE 2

Fill in the blanks with the words and phrases. Then write each sentence again using your own word or phrase. One example is below:

Check	Look at	the dialog	turns	write a paragraph
Circle	questions and answers	Think about	Work	your ideas

Example: Look at the list.
Read the list.

1. ______________ the photo.
____

2. Draw ______________.
____

3. ______________ your family.
____

4. Take ______________.
____

5. ______________ the correct answer.
____

6. Match the ______________.
____

7. Practice reading ______________.
____

8. Use complete sentences to ______________.
____

9. ______________ with a partner.
____

10. ______________ your homework.
____

PRACTICE 3

Read the situation. Choose the correct answer. Then practice saying the answer aloud.

1. **You want to show a picture to students. You say:**
   a. Look at the article.
   b. Draw your ideas.
   c. Look at the picture.

2. **You want students to tell you the vocabulary word. You say:**
   a. Look at the list.
   b. Guess the word.
   c. Play a game in pairs.

3. **You want students to find a partner and play a game. You say:**
   a. Work with a partner.
   b. Play a guessing game.
   c. Play a game in pairs.

4. **You want students to circle the right word. You say:**
   a. Circle the correct word.
   b. Guess the word.
   c. Choose words from the table.

5. **You want students to put the question with its answer. You say:**
   a. Work with a partner.
   b. Play a game in pairs.
   c. Match the questions and answers.

6. **You want students to talk about their parents. You say:**
   a. Give examples.
   b. Think about your family.
   c. Practice introducing yourself.

7. **You want students to play a game with three other students. You say:**
   a. Practice saying the description.
   b. Take turns to read the paragraph.
   c. Play in groups of four.

8. **Students read an article without a title. You say:**
   a. Choose a title for the article.
   b. Look at the title.
   c. Look at the article.

9. **A student asks, "What do we practice?" You reply:**
   a. Give instructions.
   b. Match the expressions with the pictures.
   c. Practice saying the description.

10. **You asked students to take out their notes. Now you say:**
    a. Use the picture to write a paragraph.
    b. Use your notes to write a paragraph.
    c. Give information.

REFLECT

Think about what you learned in this lesson. Write five phrases you practiced.

Phrases for Giving Activity Instructions

Now rate your confidence using these phrases. Put a check below your confidence level.

not confident	a little confident	somewhat confident	very confident

LESSON 8 GIVING ACTIVITY INSTRUCTIONS B

PREVIEW

You can give students instructions in English before activities.

In Lesson 8, you will:

- direct students to complete activities.
- explain activity instructions.
- write activity instructions clearly.
- respond to student questions on instructions.

Language to Know

chart	conversation	hobby	interview	sport
check	favorite	information	poem	

What Do You Know?

Write the phrases you know for giving activity instructions in English. Two examples are below:

Instructions for Reading and Writing	Instructions for Listening and Speaking
Write a description.	*Listen to the conversation.*

Rate your confidence using these phrases. Put a check below your confidence level.

not confident	a little confident	somewhat confident	very confident

LEARN 1

A. Here are some phrases for giving activity instructions. Listen and repeat. 4.22

Giving Activity Instructions

Listen to the teacher.

Listen and repeat.

Read about the family.

Read the description.

Read and answer the questions.

Answer the questions in complete sentences.

Repeat the sentences.

Underline the verbs.

Fill in the blanks.

Tell your classmates.

Say the word.

Ask your partner.

In pairs, talk about your family.

Talk to your partner about yourself.

Discuss the following questions.

Write a description.

Rewrite the paragraph.

In your notebook, write sentences about the pictures.

B. There are many substitutions for these phrases. Listen and repeat. 4.23

Phrases	Substitutions
Listen to the teacher.	Listen to the description/information/instructions/ conversation.
Listen and repeat.	Listen and complete the sentences. Listen and check the words you hear. Listen and choose the correct answer.
Read about the family.	Read about the sport/teacher. Read about Tom's hobbies.
Read the description.	Read the text/letter/poem/interview.
Read and answer the questions.	Read and draw a picture. Read and underline the vocabulary words.
Answer the questions in complete sentences.	Answer *yes* or *no*. Answer *true* or *false*.
Repeat the sentences.	Repeat the instructions/conversation.
Underline the verbs.	Underline the title. Underline the main idea. Underline all of the sentences with adjectives.
Fill in the blanks.	Fill in the chart. Fill in the missing letters.
Tell your classmates.	Tell the class. Tell your partner.
Say the word.	Say the letters. Say *yes* or *no*. Say *true* or *false*.
Ask your partner.	Ask each other. Ask your teacher.
In pairs, talk about your family.	With your classmates, talk about your family.
Talk to your partner about yourself.	Talk to your partner about the things in Activity 4. Talk to your partner about the people in the pictures.
Discuss the following questions.	Discuss the answers. Discuss what to do.
Write a description.	Write a list/letter. Write the words in the spaces.
In your notebook, write sentences about the pictures.	On a piece of paper, write sentences about the pictures.

LEARN 2

Read the conversation, and watch the video. Listen to a teacher give activity instructions. ▶ 4.7

Mrs. Nowak: Now, we're going to listen to descriptions of different sports around the world. Listen to the information. Then, fill in the blanks.

Jakub: Can we listen again, please?

Mrs. Nowak: Yes. Now, talk to your partner about the descriptions. Ask your partner the questions in the book about sports.

Julia: What page?

Mrs. Nowak: Page 78. In pairs, talk about these questions. Then, discuss your favorite sport with your partner.

Jakub: What's the homework?

Mrs. Nowak: On a piece of paper, write a description of your favorite sport.

PRACTICE 1

Are these instructions for writing activities or speaking activities? Write each sentence in the correct column. Then practice saying the instructions aloud.

Ask each other.
Discuss the following questions.
Fill in the blanks using the vocabulary.
On a piece of paper, answer the questions.
Repeat the sentences.
Rewrite the paragraph.
Say the word.
Talk to your partner about yourself.
Tell your classmates.
Underline the verbs.

Writing activities	Speaking activities

PRACTICE 2

Choose the correct answer.

1. **Read the ______________.**
   a. description
   b. photos
   c. family
   d. hobbies

2. **Underline the ______________.**
   a. blanks
   b. verbs
   c. class
   d. partner

3. **______________ the words.**
   a. Talk
   b. Say
   c. Listen
   d. Ask

4. **______________ a description of a sport.**
   a. Write
   b. Ask
   c. Answer
   d. Fill

5. **Listen and ______________ the conversation.**
   a. choose
   b. fill
   c. repeat
   d. answer

6. **Read ______________ the sport.**
   a. to
   b. at
   c. in
   d. about

7. **Listen ______________ the instructions.**
   a. on
   b. at
   c. with
   d. to

8. **Talk ______________ your partner about yourself.**
   a. to
   b. about
   c. at
   d. on

9. **Fill ______________ the blanks.**
   a. on
   b. in
   c. at
   d. about

10. **Answer the questions ______________ a piece of paper.**
    a. on
    b. in
    c. with
    d. about

REFLECT

Think about what you learned in this lesson. Write five phrases you practiced.

Phrases for Giving Activity Instructions

Now rate your confidence using these phrases. Put a check below your confidence level.

not confident	a little confident	somewhat confident	very confident

LESSON 9 ORGANIZING STUDENTS

PREVIEW

You can use English to organize your students before they begin activities.

In Lesson 9, you will:

- direct students to get into pairs or groups.
- tell students how much time they have for an activity.
- write instructions for organizing students.
- respond to student questions about organization.

Language to Know

alone	discussion	group	partner	until
by yourself	divide	pair	together	

What Do You Know?

Write the phrases you know for organizing students. Two examples are below:

Alone	In Pairs/Groups
Please work by yourself.	*Find a partner.*

Rate your confidence using these phrases. Put a check below your confidence level.

not confident	a little confident	somewhat confident	very confident

LEARN 1

A. Here are some phrases for organizing students. Listen and repeat. 4.24

Organizing Students

Please work by yourself.

Find a partner.

Work with a partner.

Pair up.

You can work together.

You have to get into groups of three.

Work in groups of three.

Count off by twos.

Sara, please work with Paul.

Sara and Paul, work together, please.

Sit in a circle.

Face the board.

Take turns reading the dialog.

You have five more minutes.

You have until 9:00 to finish this activity.

Paul, you are A. Sara, you are B.

This half of the class is A. This half is B.

OK, let's check. Who is A?

B. There are many substitutions for these phrases. Listen and repeat. 4.25

Phrases	Substitutions
Please work by yourself.	Please work alone. Please work on your own.
You can work together.	You can work in pairs.
You have to get into groups of three.	You have to get into pairs.
Work in groups of three.	Get into groups of three. Work in groups of four/five.
Count off by twos.	Count off by threes/fours.
Sit in a circle	Sit side by side.
Face the board.	Face each other.
Take turns reading the dialog.	Take turns answering the questions.
You have five more minutes.	You have another 10 minutes.
You have until 9:00 to finish this activity.	You have until 10:30 to finish this activity.

LEARN 2

Read the conversation, and watch the video. Listen to a teacher organize her students. 4.8

Mrs. Nowak: Today, we're going to read a conversation.
Julia: Can we work together?
Mrs. Nowak: Yes, work with a partner.
Jakub: Can I work alone?
Mrs. Nowak: No, you have to get into pairs.
Julia: Who do I work with?
Mrs. Nowak: Julia, please work with Jakub. Face each other and take turns reading the dialog. You have until 9:00 to finish this activity.
Jakub: How much time do we have?
Mrs. Nowak: You have five more minutes.

PRACTICE 1

Do these instructions ask students to work alone, in pairs, or in groups? Write each sentence in the correct column.

Count off by fours.
Pair up.
Please work on your own.
Sara, please work with Paul.
This half of the class is A. This half is B.
Find a partner.
Please work by yourself.
Sara and Paul, work together, please.
Sit in a circle.
You have to get into groups of three.

Alone	In Pairs	In Groups

PRACTICE 2

Fill in the blanks with the phrases.

9:00	alone	a partner	five more minutes	into groups of four
off by twos	of the class is A	are A	turns reading the dialog	your own

1. Please work ______________________________.
2. Find ______________________________.
3. Work on ______________________________.
4. Get ______________________________.
5. Count ______________________________.
6. Sara, you ______________________________.
7. Take ______________________________.
8. You have until ______________________________.
9. This half ______________________________.
10. You have ______________________________.

PRACTICE 3

Read the situation. Choose the correct answer. Then practice saying the answer aloud.

1. Students need a partner. You say:
   a. Pair up.
   b. Please work on your own.
   c. You are B.
   d. You have five more minutes.

2. Students have to look at the board. You say:
   a. Face each other.
   b. Face the board.
   c. Sit in a circle.
   d. Sit side by side.

3. **Students have to work alone. You say:**
   a. Find a partner.
   b. Count off by threes.
   c. Face each other.
   d. Please work by yourself.

4. **Students must finish at 3:00. You say:**
   a. You have until 3:00 to finish this activity.
   b. Please work on your own.
   c. You have another 10 minutes.
   d. You have three more minutes.

5. **Students have to finish in three minutes. You say:**
   a. You can work together.
   b. You have another five minutes.
   c. Please work on your own.
   d. You have three more minutes.

6. **Students have to take turns reading. You say:**
   a. Take turns reading the dialog.
   b. Sara and Paul, work together, please.
   c. Face the board.
   d. Count off by twos.

7. **You want to divide the class into two groups. You say:**
   a. OK, let's check. Who is A?
   b. Paul, you are A. Sara, you are B.
   c. Count off by fours.
   d. This half of the class is A. This half is B.

8. **Students have to sit next to each other. You say:**
   a. Face each other.
   b. Sit in a circle.
   c. Sit side by side.
   d. Sara, please work with Paul.

9. **Students are having a discussion in a group of three. You say:**
   a. Sit in a circle.
   b. Face the board.
   c. Sara, please work with Paul.
   d. Work with a partner.

10. **You have 16 students and you want groups of 4 students. You say:**
   a. Work in threes.
   b. Count off by fours.
   c. This half of the class is A. This half is B.
   d. Pair up.

REFLECT

Think about what you learned in this lesson. Write five phrases you practiced.

Phrases for Organizing Students

Now rate your confidence using these phrases. Put a check below your confidence level.

not confident	a little confident	somewhat confident	very confident

UNIT 5 RESEARCH BRIEF
ASSESSING STUDENT WORK: Using Formative Assessment to Correct Students

The language and routines in Unit 5 help you correct student errors in your classroom. Many teachers think of and use assessment to give grades at the end of a unit (summative assessment). Another way to assess students as they are learning is an ongoing correction (formative assessment). This gives students more chances to recognize their mistakes and improve their language.

What is formative assessment?

Formative assessment is when teachers give students feedback about their work as part of teaching the lesson. Formative assessment gives students the chance to see where they are in the learning process. Students get feedback more often. They get feedback before a summative assessment like a quiz or a test. Feedback is one kind of formative assessment that happens every day in the classroom. There are many ways teachers can give students feedback. They can identify and correct students' spoken errors during the lesson. They can identify common errors students make in written homework. They can correct those errors in "real time." This gives the student a chance to try again and to fix their own mistakes.

Why does formative assessment matter?

When teachers use formative assessment strategies like feedback, they can see how much the students understand. They can then adjust[1] the lesson to help students learn. Assessing students while they are learning can help the teachers notice problems and prepare lessons to support students.

Formative assessment is also good for students because it gives them many chances to correct what they are doing while they are learning. The more times teachers assess students while they are learning, the more chances students have to improve their work.

A research study

TYPES OF FEEDBACK

In a study of Japanese university students learning English, Ellis, Sheen, Murakami, and Takashima (2008) describe four types of feedback: *direct* or *indirect* and *focused* or *unfocused*. They describe how feedback that helps students self-correct can have different purposes.

Direct feedback gives students the answer and asks them to correct their work. This type of feedback can help students practice a new language form over and over. Indirect feedback points students in the direction of the answer and asks them to correct their work. This type of feedback can help students practice and self-correct a language form they have already learned.

Unfocused feedback asks students to correct every error. This type of feedback is good for editing a final piece of writing. Focused feedback asks students to correct only the errors related to the language form(s) students are actively learning in the task. This type of feedback is helpful for understanding and learning a language form.

[1] adjust: to change

Researchers questions and findings

Below are some questions researchers have asked about formative assessment. Findings of these studies are listed after each question.

1. **How do teachers give students written and spoken feedback?**
   Feedback can be

   a. direct or indirect feedback and focused or unfocused to help students see and self-correct their errors (See A research study: Types of Feedback, Ellis, Sheen, Murakami, & Takashima, 2008).

   b. in the form of recasts (repeating the answer correctly), explicit[2] correction, elicitation (asking students to correct the error), clarification (asking the student to explain), repeating the error, or teaching about the error (Lyster & Ranta, 1997).

   c. used differently depending on the students' language level (Nemati, Alavi, & Mohebbi, 2019).

2. **How do students respond to formative feedback?**
   Students

   a. feel more independent and correct their own work instead of the teacher doing the correcting (Chan & Lam, 2010; Crooks, 1988; Nicol & Macfarlane-Dick, 2006).

   b. are less frustrated because they expect feedback from teachers (Ferris, 1995; Leki, 1991).

   c. increase their metalinguistic knowledge—their knowledge *about* language—while they also increase how well they use the language (Ellis et al., 2008).

3. **How do chances for students to correct their work help them learn?**
   Students

   a. get feedback on their work as they are developing their skills. Written corrective feedback gives students individual feedback on their specific language errors. Spoken corrective feedback gives students a chance to correct their mistakes when they make the error, not later (Lee, 2013; Sheen, 2010).

   b. improve on the language feature they are learning (Bitchener, 2008).

   c. produce language—additional chances for producing language are very important for language learning (Swain, 1993, 2005).

   d. repair errors that they make often by practicing self-correction (Tsang, 2004).

---

[2] explicit: clear, direct

UNIT 5 ASSESSING STUDENT WORK

LESSON 1 IDENTIFYING AND CORRECTING WRITTEN ERRORS

PREVIEW

You can identify and correct errors that students make in writing.

In Lesson 1, you will:
- identify common writing errors.
- write corrections for errors in grammar.
- write corrections for errors in spelling and punctuation.

Language to Know

capitalization	nationality	period	plural	punctuation
shy	spelling	thin	vacuum	

What Do You Know?

Some written errors are easier to identify than others. Write E for *Easy to identify* or D for *Difficult to identify*.

1. ______________ spelling
2. ______________ plural forms
3. ______________ punctuation
4. ______________ verb use
5. ______________ capitalization
6. ______________ past tense forms

LEARN 1

A teacher is correcting grammar. Look at the activity in the student book. Then look at the teacher's corrections of the student's sentences.

Grammar Exercise: Past Simple of the Verb *be*

Past Simple of the Verb *be*		
	Affirmative	**Negative**
I He She It	was	was not
We You They	were	were not

A. Rewrite the sentences in the simple past.

1. Anna is in high school.

 ____

2. Your parents are sports fans.

 ____

3. Their friends are not in class.

 ____

4. Jeff and Debra are in Scotland.

 ____

Aisha

English Homework

✓ 1. Anna was in high school.

2. Your parents ^ sports fans.
were

3. Their friends were ~~no~~ in class.
not

4. Jeff and Debra ~~was~~ in Scotland.
were

LEARN 2

A teacher is correcting spelling, punctuation, and capitalization. Look at the activity in the student book and the rules. Then look at the teacher's corrections of the student's sentences.

Lesson 15: Household Chores

A. Study the sentence model.

subject + verb + object + time phrase

B. Look at the household chores.

make the bed	vacuum the floor
do the laundry	take out the trash
wash the dishes	set the table

C. Look at the time phrases.

often	never	sometimes
every day	yesterday	today
this morning	next year	every week

D. Write about household chores. Use complete sentences with time phrases.

Example: *I make my bed every morning.*

1. ______________________________

2. ______________________________

RULES

Spelling:

- Add *-s* to make most nouns plural.
- Add *-es* to words ending in *sh* and *ch* to make plurals.
- Drop silent *e* before adding *-ing*.

Punctuation:

- Use a period (.) at the end of a sentence.

Capitalization:

- Capitalize the first word of a sentence.
- Capitalize names of people and special places.

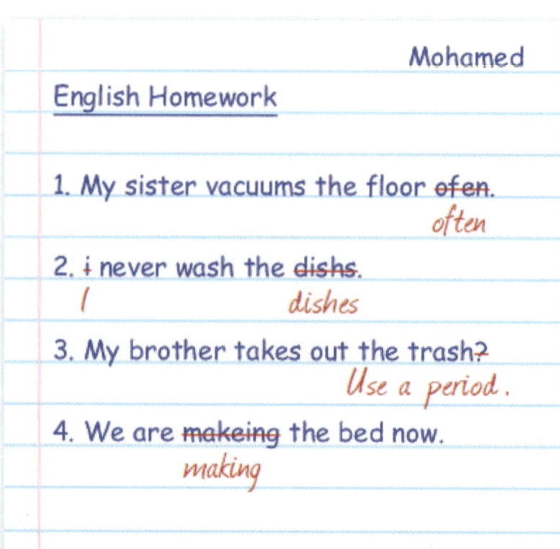

Mohamed

English Homework

1. My sister vacuums the floor ~~ofen~~. often
2. ~~i~~ never wash the ~~dishs~~. I dishes
3. My brother takes out the trash~~?~~ Use a period.
4. We are ~~makeing~~ the bed now. making

PRACTICE 1

Identify the kind of error. Write *S* for *spelling*, *G* for *grammar*, and *P* for *punctuation*. Then correct the errors.

1. ______________ I don't like pizza
2. ______________ Lets go to the park.
3. ______________ He were at the movies.
4. ______________ They are writeing.
5. ______________ Do you do the dishs?
6. ______________ His name is John,
7. ______________ Can we go home now.
8. ______________ I never takes out the trash.

PRACTICE 2

Read the student's homework. Find and correct the 10 errors. There are errors in spelling, punctuation, and grammar. Write the corrections above the errors.

My To Friends

I have two good freinds. their names are Meryem and Nebila. Meryem having long, brown hair. She is taller and thiner than Nebila. she is also quieter. Nebila's hair was shorter and darker then Meryem's hair? Nebila is funnyer than Meryem. I like Meryem and Nebila very much.

REFLECT

How confident are you correcting students' written errors? Write C for *Confident*, SC for *Somewhat Confident*, or NC for *Not Confident*.

1. ______________ spelling
2. ______________ plural forms
3. ______________ punctuation
4. ______________ verb use
5. ______________ capitalization
6. ______________ past tense verbs

LESSON 2 IDENTIFYING AND CORRECTING SPOKEN ERRORS

PREVIEW

You can identify and correct students' spoken errors. A useful technique is to repeat items correctly.

In Lesson 2, you will:
- listen for spoken errors.
- identify common types of spoken errors.
- model correct speech for spoken errors.

Language to Know

missing	model	preposition	pronoun	pronunciation

What Do You Know?

Some spoken errors are easier to identify than others. Write each type of error in one of the columns.

adding extra words	preposition use	pronunciation	vocabulary use
leaving words out	pronoun use	verb tense	word order

Easy to Identify	Difficult to Identify

Rate your confidence identifying spoken errors. Put a check below your confidence level.

not confident	a little confident	somewhat confident	very confident

LEARN 1

Read the conversation, and watch the video. Listen to the teacher correct the spoken errors. ▶ 5.1

Mr. Khaled: I need two volunteers to practice introducing themselves.
Mohamed: I can do it.
Mr. Khaled: Thank you, Mohamed. Please come to the front. One more volunteer… Thank you, Sharif. Please stand with Mohamed. Let's begin.
Mohamed: Hello. What is your name?
Sharif: I name is Sharif.
Mr. Khaled: My name is Sharif. Please repeat.
Sharif: My name is Sharif.
Mohamed: I am Mohamed. How old you?
Mr. Khaled: How old are you?
Mohamed: How old are you?
Sharif: I am 12.
Mohamed: I am 12, too.

PRACTICE 1

These sentences are incorrect. Correct the sentences and write them in the correct column.

Did you went?
It's warm and sun.
This is new computer.
How much does cost?
My name Julia.
We are happiness.
How old you are now?
She cats doesn't like.
It's a blue, new pen.
She do not like to skate.

Word Is Incorrect	Word Is Missing	Word Order Is Incorrect

PRACTICE 2

Fill in the blanks with the words to complete the teacher's corrections.

Are	don't	in	of all	the
didn't	has	isn't	play	time

1. **Student:** I no have a brother.
   Teacher: I _______ have a brother.
2. **Student:** Does Mohamed sports?
   Teacher: Does Mohamed _______ sports?
3. **Student:** Aisha going to the party.
   Teacher: Aisha _______ going to the party.
4. **Student:** We going shopping?
   Teacher: _______ we going shopping?
5. **Student:** We visited museum this afternoon.
   Teacher: We visited _______ museum this afternoon.
6. **Student:** Fatima have black hair.
   Teacher: Fatima _______ black hair.
7. **Student:** Excuse me. What hour is it?
   Teacher: What _______ is it?
8. **Student:** My birthday is on February.
   Teacher: My birthday is _______ February.
9. **Student:** You no go to the library.
   Teacher: You _______ go to the library.
10. **Student:** I take care all of my children's needs.
    Teacher: I take care _______ my children's needs.

PRACTICE 3

Fill in the blanks with the words and phrases. Then practice the teacher's lines.

after me	have	let's practice	repeat	Very good

Teacher: Now _______ the conversation. Please begin.
Student A: Do you have any brother?

Teacher: Do you have any brothers? Please _______.

Student A: Do you have any brothers?
Teacher: _______. Continue please.

Student B: Yes, I one brother have.
Teacher: I _______ one brother.

Student A: What his name?
Teacher: Repeat _______. What is his name?

Student A: What is his name?

REFLECT

How confident are you correcting students' spoken errors? Write each type of error in one of the columns.

adding extra words	preposition use	pronunciation	vocabulary use
leaving words out	pronoun use	verb tense	word order

Confident	Somewhat Confident	Not Confident

Now rate your confidence correcting spoken errors. Put a check below your confidence level.

not confident	a little confident	somewhat confident	very confident

LESSON 3 ASSESSING STUDENT COMPREHENSION

PREVIEW

You can check your students' comprehension of reading and listening content.

In Lesson 3, you will:

- use spoken and written questions to assess comprehension.
- read written work to assess comprehension.
- listen to spoken responses to assess comprehension.

Language to Know

burning	coin	drawing	germ	summarize
cage	danger	fire	orally	

What Do You Know?

How do you assess students' comprehension? Write each method in one of the columns: *Often*, *Sometimes*, or *Rarely*.

asking questions about content
checking student homework
giving quizzes
giving tests
having students ask each other questions
having students make a drawing
having students summarize the lesson in writing
having students summarize the lesson orally
reading student writing

Often	Sometimes	Rarely

Rate your confidence assessing students' comprehension. Put a check below your confidence level.

not confident	a little confident	somewhat confident	very confident

LEARN 1

Read the conversation, and watch the video. Listen to a teacher check students' comprehension. ▶ 5.2

Mr. Khaled: Please turn to page 34. Let's discuss the story that you read yesterday.
Mohamed: Excuse me. What page?
Mr. Khaled: Page 34. Who can tell me what happened? Mohamed?
Mohamed: A lion caught a mouse and let him go.
Mr. Khaled: Very good. Why did the lion let the mouse go?
Sharif: The mouse ran away.
Mr. Khaled: That's not quite right. Does anyone know the answer?
Mr. Khaled: Let's listen to the story.
Narrator: The mouse said, "Let me go and I promise you that someday I will help you." The lion thought this was funny, and so he decided to let the mouse go. The next day, the lion got caught in a hunter's net.
Mr. Khaled: What did the lion think about the mouse's answer? Anyone?
Mohamed: He thought it was funny.
Mr. Khaled: Excellent! Then, what happened to the lion?

PRACTICE 1

Read the passage. Then read a teacher's conversation with a student. Answer *Yes* or *No* to each question.

My Coin Collection
by Bill Jones

I have over 700 coins! They are from faraway countries that my father visits. My father gives them to me. Some are square. Some have holes in the middle! Some have pictures of queens, kings, presidents, or even animals. One from Australia has a koala bear on it. I put all my coins in a coin book. The book protects them, and it's easier to see them all.

1. **Teacher:** What does Bill collect?
   Student: Coins.
   Is the student's answer correct? ____________________

2. **Teacher:** How many coins does Bill have?
   Student: 600.
   Is the student's answer correct? ____________________

3. **Teacher:** Where are the coins from?
   Student: A country.
   Is the student's answer correct? ____________________

4. **Teacher:** Who gives the coins to Bill?
   Student: Queens and kings.
   Is the student's answer correct? ____________________

5. **Teacher:** What shape are some of the coins?
   Student: Square.
   Is the student's answer correct? ____________________

6. **Teacher:** Who is often on a coin?
Student: A queen, king, president, or animal.

Is the student's answer correct?
____

7. **Teacher:** What animal is on the Australian coin?
Student: Panda bear.

Is the student's answer correct?
____

8. **Teacher:** Where does Bill put the coins?
Student: In a coin book.

Is the student's answer correct?
____

9. **Teacher:** Are the coins protected?
Student: No, they're not.

Is the student's answer correct?
____

10. **Teacher:** Can Bill see all of the coins?
Student: Yes, he can.

Is the student's answer correct?
____

PRACTICE 2

Read the passage. Then read a teacher's conversation with a student. Choose the correct answer for each question.

Stay Healthy

It is not fun being sick. You have to stay home. You can't play with your friends. Do these things to stay healthy:

1. Wash your hands often. Use hot water and soap. Wash for 20 seconds to kill the germs.
2. Get sleep. Get 7 to 8 hours every night to help your body fight sickness.
3. Never sneeze in your hand! Germs go on anything you touch. If you get a cold, sneeze into your arm to keep your family and friends healthy.

1. **Teacher:** What do you have to do if you are sick?
Student: Play with your friends.

Is the student's answer correct?
a. The answer is correct.
b. The answer is incorrect. Answer: You have to stay home, and you can't play with your friends.
c. The answer is incorrect. Answer: There are some things you can do to stay healthy.

2. **Teacher:** What is one thing you can do to stay healthy?
Student: Wash your hands.

Is the student's answer correct?
a. The answer is correct.
b. The answer is incorrect. Answer: Put germs on anything you touch.
c. The answer is incorrect. Answer: Sneeze into your hand.

3. **Teacher:** How long should you wash your hands?
Student: 20 minutes.

Is the student's answer correct?
a. The answer is correct.
b. The answer is incorrect. Answer: 20 seconds.
c. The answer is incorrect. Answer: 7 to 8 hours.

4. **Teacher:** What is another way to stay healthy?
Student: Get sleep.

Is the student's answer correct?
a. The answer is correct.
b. The answer is incorrect. Answer: You have to stay home.
c. The answer is incorrect. Answer: Sneeze into your arm.

5. **Teacher:** How does sleep help you?
Student: 7 to 8 hours.

Is the student's answer correct?
a. The answer is correct.
b. The answer is incorrect. Answer: Sleep helps your body fight sickness.
c. The answer is incorrect. Answer: It's important to get sleep.

6. **Teacher:** How many hours of sleep should you get a night?
Student: 20 hours.

Is the student's answer correct?
a. The answer is correct.
b. The answer is incorrect. Answer: Getting enough sleep helps your body fight sickness.
c. The answer is incorrect. Answer: 7 to 8 hours a night.

7. **Teacher:** Where should you sneeze?
Student: You should sneeze into your hand.

Is the student's answer correct?
a. The answer is correct.
b. The answer is incorrect. Answer: You should sneeze into your arm.
c. The answer is incorrect. Answer: You should sneeze on your family and friends.

8. **Teacher:** What happens if you sneeze into your hand?
Student: Family and friends can stay healthy.

Is the student's answer correct?
a. The answer is correct.
b. The answer is incorrect. Answer: Germs go on your arm.
c. The answer is incorrect. Answer: The germs go on anything you touch.

9. **Teacher:** Why is it no fun being sick?
Student: Because you like to sneeze.

Is the student's answer correct?
a. The answer is correct.
b. The answer is incorrect. Answer: Because you have to wash your hands every 20 seconds.
c. The answer is incorrect. Answer: Because you have to stay home, and you can't play with your friends.

10. **Teacher:** Why do you think this was written?
Student: To tell people how to stay healthy.

Is the student's answer correct?
a. The answer is correct.
b. The answer is incorrect. Answer: To tell people what to do when they sneeze.
c. The answer is incorrect. Answer: To tell people to sleep less.

REFLECT

How confident are you assessing students' comprehension? Write each method in one of the columns: *Confident*, *Somewhat Confident*, or *Not Confident*.

asking questions about content
checking student homework
giving quizzes
giving tests
having students ask each other questions
having students make a drawing
having students summarize the lesson in writing
having students summarize the lesson orally
reading student writing

Confident	Somewhat Confident	Not Confident

Now rate your confidence using these phrases. Put a check below your confidence level.

not confident	a little confident	somewhat confident	very confident

UNIT 4 REVIEW

1 Read the chart. Then underline the errors in the student's sentences. Correct each error. There is one error in each sentence.

Comparative Adjectives
nice → nicer easy → easier big → bigger

1. This towel is softer and niceer than that towel.
2. My sister is funnyier than me.
3. My sister is fitter and braveer than my brother.
4. Yesterday was cloudier than today, but also hoter.
5. That supermarket is larger and busyer than this one.

2 Read the chart. Then underline and correct the errors in the conversation. There are six errors.

Wh- Questions with *do*
What color hair do you have? When does he go to class? Where do they live?

Student A: What color hair does your brothers having?

Student B: Their hair is brown.

Student A: What do your sister looking like?

Student B: She is tall, and she has black hair.

Student A: Where she does go to school?

3 Read the passage. Then complete the conversation with phrases from the box.

Reading Passage

Sara is very excited. She is going to visit her grandparents. They live in a big city, and there are lots of fun things to do in the city. Sara wants to go to the zoo. Then she wants to visit the museums.

How does she feel	She's going to visit her grandparents	What is she going to do
Who is Sara	Why is she excited	

Teacher: ________________________________?
Aisha: A girl. The story is about her.

Teacher: That's right. ________________________________?
Aisha: Visiting grandparents.

Teacher: ________________________________.
Aisha: She's going to visit her grandparents.

Teacher: Good. ________________________________?
Fatima: She is very exciting.

Teacher: She is very excited. ________________________________?
Fatima: Because her grandparents live in a big city.

4 Look at the errors in the student's response. Complete the passage with the correct answers.

STUDENT'S RESPONSE

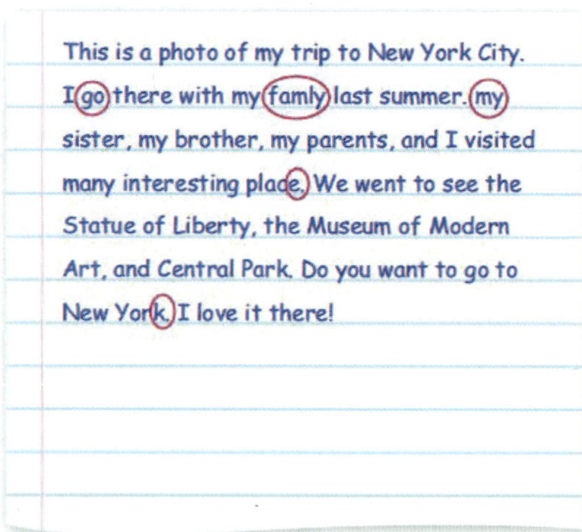
This is a photo of my trip to New York City.
I go there with my famly last summer. my
sister, my brother, my parents, and I visited
many interesting place. We went to see the
Statue of Liberty, the Museum of Modern
Art, and Central Park. Do you want to go to
New York. I love it there!

This is a photo of my trip to New York City. I ____________ there with my ____________ last summer. ____________ sister, my brother, my parents, and I visited many interesting ____________. We went to see the Statue of Liberty, the Museum of Modern Art, and Central Park. Do you want to go to New York ____________ I love it there!

5 **Read the situation and the activity in the textbook. Then read the teacher's conversation with a student. Choose the correct response for the teacher.**

1. Situation: You are checking comprehension of the dialog and identifying students' spoken errors.

CONVERSATION

Jim: Hi, John. How are you?
John: Hello, Jim! I'm great. I'm going to visit a university tomorrow.
Jim: That's exciting! Who are you going with?
John: I'm going with my friend, Karl.

Teacher: Where is John going?
Student: He is going to visit his friend.
Teacher: ______________________________

a. No, that's not right.
b. Try again. Very good. Thank you.
c. What is his friend's name?
d. He is visiting his friend. Please repeat.

2. Situation: The class is practicing spelling. You are identifying and correcting written errors.

CHART IN TEXTBOOK

i* before *e* except after *c	
belief	ceiling
field	receive

Teacher: Please say your sentence and write it on the board.
Student writes: I recieve many phone calls.
Teacher: ______________________________

a. Who can tell me what happened?
b. That's not correct. Please spell "phone."
c. I asked you to write the sentence.
d. That's incorrect. Please spell "receive."

3. Situation: You are explaining pronouns. You are checking comprehension and identifying and correcting spoken errors.

CHART IN TEXTBOOK

Pronouns
Did you eat the pie?
Yes! The pie was amazing!
Yes! It was amazing!

Teacher: Did you like the movie?
Student: No. I was very boring.
Teacher: ______________________________

a. You didn't see the movie.
b. It was boring. Repeat please.
c. I'm happy you liked it.
d. No, you didn't. You were boring.

4. Situation: Students are writing sentences with gerunds. You are identifying and correcting written errors.

CHART IN TEXTBOOK

Likes and Dislikes
I enjoy playing soccer. I dislike studying.

Teacher: Read your sentence please.
Student: I dislike to play the piano.
Teacher: ______________________________

a. You don't have a piano.
b. You enjoy playing the piano.
c. You dislike playing the piano.
d. You never play the piano.

5. Situation: The class has finished reading the story. You are asking questions to check comprehension and get student responses.

READING IN TEXTBOOK

Last fall, I joined the basketball team. We practiced every day, but we never won any games. Last Friday, we played our last game of the term. We were feeling sad, but we played our best. Do you know what happened? We won!

Teacher: ______________________________
Student: The boy's team won the game.
Teacher: That's right.

a. Where does the boy go to high school?
b. How do you play basketball?
c. Who played on the basketball team?
d. What happened at the end of the story?

UNIT 6 RESEARCH BRIEF
GIVING FEEDBACK: Encouraging Student Independence

The language and routines in Unit 6 help you to give feedback to motivate student learning and encourage students to self-correct. This helps students set goals and have more control over their learning and be more independent.

What is feedback?

In the classroom, feedback is information the teacher gives a student about their work or performance on a task. When teachers set clear criteria[1] for a task, feedback can help students compare their work with the learning goal. Teacher feedback can also help the student to see how to improve on the task so the student can self-correct to meet the goals of the task.

Why is feedback important for learning?

Research shows that students learn better when they receive feedback that provides them with information about how to make their work better. Many research studies have shown that feedback can have an effect on students, but depending on the feedback, the effect can help or get in the way of[2] learning.

Positive feedback encourages student motivation. Motivation is the desire to reach a goal. It can affect how hard students try, how much anxiety[3] they feel, and how well they learn language in the classroom. Learning a language can make some students feel uncomfortable. When students get positive feedback as they are practicing the language, they are more likely to be motivated to continue learning.

Explicit[4] feedback provides information that helps students correct their own work. When students take on more responsibility for their learning, they learn skills to help them study and practice the language outside of the classroom and later in life. The goal is for students to learn to work independently so that they do not always need the teacher to correct every error.

A research study

THE POWER OF FEEDBACK

Hattie & Timperley (2007) state that feedback should answer three important questions for the student who is working toward a goal: (1) Where am I going? (2) How am I going? and (3) Where to next?

"Where am I going?" helps students understand the goals of the task. It is important that the goals and steps are clear to students. It is easier for students to understand the next steps if they understand the goal and all the activities to get to the goal.

"How am I going?" helps students see what progress they have made. It answers how they are doing on the task so far. It is helpful when the feedback comes before a final test or quiz so students can make changes. It is best when the feedback is specific (not general) so students know where to focus.

"Where to next?" is the question that helps students understand the next steps. This question helps students see the activities they should do to work toward the goal. "Where to next?" tells students if they need to make changes to their work. It helps them work more independently.

Feedback that answers all three questions is helpful, but feedback that answers the "where to next" question "can have some of the most powerful impacts on learning" (p. 90). This type of feedback helps students take control, self-regulate, and self-correct. These skills help them on the task, but also as learners in general.

[1] criteria: conditions; expectations
[2] get in the way of: to interrupt; block
[3] anxiety: worry; stress
[4] explicit: direct, clear

Research questions and findings

Below are some questions researchers have asked about how feedback can help students. Findings of these studies are listed after each question.

1. **What makes feedback helpful for students?**
   Feedback is helpful

   a. when it comes during the task or soon after, and students have the chance to correct their errors (Crooks, 1988).

   b. when it relates directly to the task and clearly explains how to do the task better. Feedback is less helpful when it is general or unclear what the student should do to improve (Hattie & Timperley, 2007).

   c. when it helps students improve their work and take control of their own learning (Black & Wiliam, 2009).

   d. when it is about the individual student's work and progress, not when it compares one student to another student (Ames & Ames, 1981).

2. **What is the relationship between feedback and motivation?**
   Feedback helps student motivation

   a. when it gives students clear strategies and steps in the right direction and gives them control, not when it does the work for them (Hattie & Timperley, 2007). Giving students control and chances to try again motivates students to work on a task because they want to (intrinsic motivation), not because they must (extrinsic motivation) (Deci, Koestner, & Ryan, 1999; Fong, Patall, Vasquez, & Stautberg, 2019).

   b. when it is formative, and students have the chance to improve their work before the quiz or test (Chan & Lam 2010).

   c. when it is positive. (Negative feedback can affect student motivation negatively because students may think of feedback only as an embarrassing experience.) (Baron, 1988; Chan & Lam, 2010).

   d. when it praises[5] effort or determination[6] at the task, not when it praises intelligence or other student characteristics (Dweck, Davidson, Nelson, & Enna, 1978).

3. **What happens when teacher feedback helps students to self-correct their work?**
   Students

   a. have more motivation, commitment, control, and confidence in a task (Hattie & Timperley, 2007; Noels, Clément, & Pelletier, 1999).

   b. begin to set their own goals, choose their own strategies, and work toward those goals independently (Butler & Winne, 1995).

   c. work harder and longer even when they face challenges (Chan & Lam, 2010).

[5] praise: to express admiration for, say something is good
[6] determination: the ability to continue at something

UNIT 6 GIVING FEEDBACK

LESSON 1 GIVING POSITIVE FEEDBACK

PREVIEW

You can give students feedback on their work in English. When you give positive feedback, you support and encourage their learning.

In Lesson 1, you will:

- tell students that you like their work.
- give positive feedback clearly.
- write positive comments on student work.
- respond to student comments.

Language to Know

everyone	irregular	positive	verb
feedback	past tense	ready	workbook

What Do You Know?

Write the words or phrases you know for giving positive feedback. One example is below:

Well done!

Rate your confidence using these phrases. Put a check below your confidence level.

not confident	a little confident	somewhat confident	very confident

LEARN 1

Here are some phrases for giving positive feedback. Listen and repeat. 6.1

Giving Positive Feedback

Good!

Good job!

Very good.

Great.

Excellent.

Nice work.

Well done!

OK!

Right!

That's right!

LEARN 2

Read the conversation, and watch the video. Listen to the teacher give positive feedback. 6.1

Mrs. Sato: Nice work. Now, let's review the irregular verbs from the homework. When I say a verb, you will tell me the past tense form. Are you ready?

Class: Yes.

Mrs. Sato: The first verb is "go." Yumi?

Yumi: "Went."

Mrs. Sato: Good! The next verb is "eat." Takeshi?

Takeshi: "Ate."

Mrs. Sato: Very good! "See"?

Yumi: "Saw."

Mrs. Sato: That's right! "Write"?

Takeshi: "Wrote."

Mrs. Sato: Excellent! Well done, everyone!

PRACTICE 1

Choose the correct answer.

1. **Good ______________!**
   a. done
   b. job
   c. right
   d. very

2. **Well ______________!**
   a. right
   b. job
   c. work
   d. done

3. **Nice ______________!**
   a. work
   b. done
   c. excellent
   d. good

4. **That's ______________!**
   a. work
   b. very
   c. right
   d. well

5. **Very ______________.**
   a. work
   b. good
   c. great
   d. right

6. **Excellent. ______________ done!**
   a. Very
   b. Great
   c. Well
   d. Right

7. **Good! ______________ work.**
   a. Nice
   b. That's
   c. Well
   d. Right

8. **Right! ______________.**
   a. Work
   b. Job
   c. Well
   d. Great

9. **That's right! ______________.**
   a. Very
   b. Right
   c. Excellent
   d. Well

10. **______________! Very good.**
    a. Done
    b. Well
    c. OK
    d. Job

PRACTICE 2

Write the correct letters or words in the blanks to complete the phrases for positive feedback.

1. O ______________!
2. G ______________!
3. Gr ______________.
4. R ______________!
5. V______________ g ______________.
6. E ______________.
7. G______________ j ______________!
8. N ______________ ______________.
9. W ______________ ______________!
10. T______________ ______________!

REFLECT

Think about what you learned in this lesson. Write five phrases you practiced.

Phrases for Giving Positive Feedback

Now rate your confidence using these phrases. Put a check below your confidence level.

not confident	a little confident	somewhat confident	very confident

LESSON 2 ENCOURAGING SELF-CORRECTION A

PREVIEW

You can encourage your students to correct their own errors in English. When your students learn to self-correct, they depend less on your feedback.

In Lesson 2, you will:

- tell students when they make errors.
- help students self-correct in class.
- write suggestions for self-corrections.
- respond to students' questions.

Language to Know

encourage	example	extra	incomplete	incorrect	missing	self-correct

What Do You Know?

Do you know these phrases for helping students self-correct? Write each phrase in one of the columns.

Don't forget to follow the example.	Do you mean "like" or "liked"?	Something is missing.
That's incorrect.	That's not quite right.	There are extra words here.
There's a problem with this paragraph.	This word is not clear.	This word is wrong.
What does this mean?		

Know	Don't Know

Rate your confidence using these phrases. Put a check below your confidence level.

not confident	a little confident	somewhat confident	very confident

LEARN 1

A. Here are some phrases for encouraging self-correction. Listen and repeat. 6.2

Encouraging Self-Correction

That isn't correct.

That's incorrect.

That's not quite right.

This word is wrong.

Something is missing.

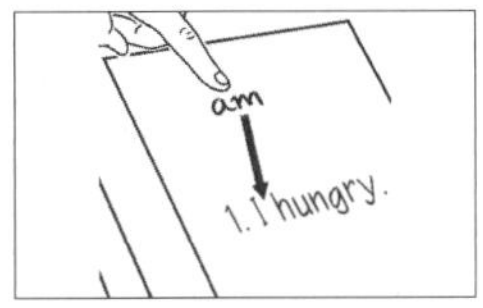

Add another word.

Use another verb.

Don't add another word.

There's an extra word here.

There are extra words here.

What does this mean?

Do you mean "like" or "liked"?

I think you're trying to say "liked," not "likes."

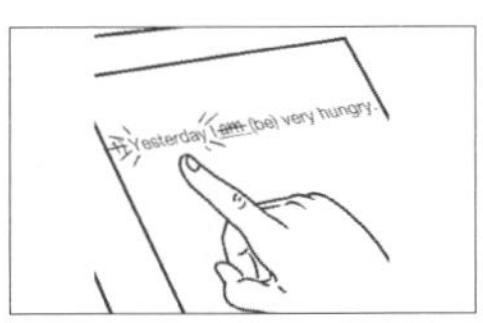

Remember we're talking about the past.

There's a problem with this sentence.

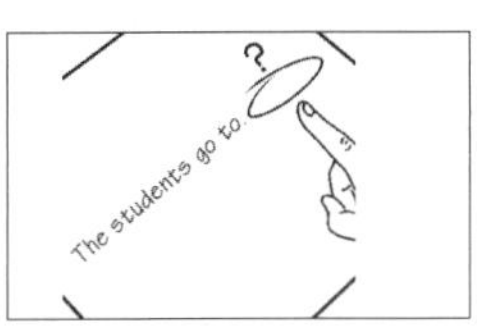

This sentence is incomplete.

Don't forget to follow the word order in the example.

B. There are many substitutions for these phrases. Listen and repeat. 6.3

Phrases	Substitutions
This word is wrong.	Your verb is wrong. This answer is wrong.
Something is missing.	A word is missing. The verb is missing.
Add another word.	Add another verb. Add a sentence.
Use another verb.	Use another word. Use the past tense.
Don't add another word.	Don't use "the."
I think you're trying to say "liked," not "likes."	I think you're trying to say "going," not "goes."
Remember we're talking about the past.	Remember we're talking about animals.
There's a problem with this sentence.	There's a problem with these words. There's a problem with this paragraph.
This sentence is incomplete.	This answer is incomplete. This sentence is wrong. This sentence is incorrect.
Don't forget to follow the word order in the example.	Remember to follow the word order in the example. Don't forget to follow the chart/example/ instructions.

LEARN 2

Read the conversation, and watch the video. Listen to a teacher encourage self-correction. 6.2

Mrs. Sato: Now we are going to practice plurals. Please look at your workbooks. Takeshi, please do number 1.
Takeshi: "There are the two plate."
Mrs. Sato: That's not quite right. Think about the plural form. Something is missing. Don't forget to follow the example.
Takeshi: "There are the two plates."
Mrs. Sato: Good, but there is one more problem. There's an extra word here.
Takeshi: Oh! "There are two plates."
Mrs. Sato: Excellent. Yumi, can you read the next one?
Yumi: "There are two dish."
Mrs. Sato: That's incorrect. Try adding *-es*.
Yumi: "There are two dishes."
Mrs. Sato: Yes! Very good.

PRACTICE 1

Choose the correct answer.

1. **That ____________ correct.**
   a. trying
   b. use
   c. isn't
   d. word

2. **Your ____________ is wrong.**
   a. sentence
   b. extra
   c. mean
   d. past

3. **____________ to add *-es*.**
   a. Don't
   b. I think
   c. Use
   d. Remember

4. **What does this ____________?**
   a. is
   b. mean
   c. forget
   d. remember

5. **Don't forget to ____________ the instructions.**
   a. be
   b. add
   c. follow
   d. mean

6. **There's a problem with ____________.**
   a. past verb
   b. this paragraph
   c. wrong sentence
   d. add *-ed*

7. **____________ "why" or "because"?**
   a. What does
   b. Do you
   c. Do you mean
   d. Do you follow

8. **There are ____________. Don't add another word.**
   a. another word
   b. extra words here
   c. instructions
   d. not quite right

9. **Remember, ____________ family.**
   a. We're talking about
   b. there's a problem
   c. the word order
   d. to follow the example

10. **Use the past tense. Don't forget ____________.**
   a. That's incorrect
   b. this word is wrong
   c. there's an extra word here
   d. to add *-ed*

PRACTICE 2

Read the student's responses. Then fill in the blanks with the sentences to encourage self-correction.

Add *-es*.	Don't add "the."
Don't use *-es*.	Do you mean "girl" or "girls?"
Remember to use *-ies* for words ending in *-y*.	There's a problem with this verb.
There's a word missing.	This sentence is incomplete.
Use "is" with "he" or "she."	What does this mean?

1. There are two box.

2. I three books.

3. The man put.

4. We have the fun.

5. I have two balles.

6. She are happy.

7. Tired apples.

8. She have two cups.

9. The girls has a doll.

10. They visit four city.

PRACTICE 3

Read the answer key and the student's response. Then choose the correct feedback.

1. **ANSWER KEY:**
   Answer: There are six classes.
   Student's Response
   There is six classes.
   a. Try adding "is."
   b. This verb is wrong.
   a. Don't add *-es*.

2. **ANSWER KEY:**
   Answer: I like to play basketball.
   Student's Response
   I like play basketball.
   a. Do you mean "play" or "plays"?
   b. There's an extra word.
   c. Add "to."

3. **ANSWER KEY:**
   Answer: She has five books.
   Student's Response
   She has the five books.
   a. The verb is wrong.
   b. There's an extra word here.
   c. Don't forget to add *-s*.

4. **ANSWER KEY:**
   Answer: There are many boys in the class.
   Student's Response
   There are many boy in the class.
   a. Add another verb.
   b. Something is missing.
   c. Don't add *-s*.

5. **ANSWER KEY:**

   Answer: She goes to art class.

   Student's Response

   She goes to are class.

   a. A word is missing.

   b. The word is incorrect.

   c. Add "the."

6. **ANSWER KEY:**

   Answer: He is happy.

   Student's Response

   He is the happy.

   a. A word is missing.

   b. There's an extra word.

   c. I think you're trying to say "happier."

7. **ANSWER KEY:**

   Answer: We are going to school.

   Student's Response

   We are going to.

   a. There's a problem with this paragraph.

   b. There are extra words here.

   c. This sentence is incomplete.

8. **ANSWER KEY:**

   Answer: The man went home.

   Student's Response

   The home went the man.

   a. Do you mean "homes"?

   b. What does this mean?

   c. A word is missing.

9. **ANSWER KEY:**

   Answer: The man painted a picture.

   Student's Response

   The man paint a picture.

   a. Don't use *-ed*. Remember we're talking about the past.

   b. I think you're trying to say "paints," not "paint."

   c. Remember to use "painted" to talk about the past.

10. **ANSWER KEY:**

    Answer: The children are loud.

    Student's Response

    Loud the children.

    a. I think you're trying to say, "child."

    b. Remember, we're talking about children.

    c. There's a problem with this sentence.

REFLECT

Think about what you learned in this lesson. Write five phrases you practiced.

Phrases for Encouraging Self-Correction

Now rate your confidence using these phrases. Put a check below your confidence level.

not confident	a little confident	somewhat confident	very confident

LESSON 3 ENCOURAGING SELF-CORRECTION B

PREVIEW

You can help your students recognize their errors in English. They will be able to self-correct and work independently.

In Lesson 3, you will:

- direct students to find their errors.
- ask questions to help students self-correct.
- write suggestions for self-correction.
- respond to students' questions.

Language to Know

chart	encourage	model	self-correct
compare	information	order	tense

What Do You Know?

Do you know these phrases to help students self-correct? Write *K* if you know the phrase. Write *DK* if you do not know the phrase.

_______________ What's missing?

_______________ What is wrong with this sentence?

_______________ Does this word look right?

_______________ Check spelling.

_______________ Try adding another verb.

_______________ Please look at this example again.

_______________ Compare the difference between "like" and "likes."

_______________ This sentence is off topic.

_______________ Pay attention to the instructions.

_______________ Please revise this sentence.

Rate your confidence using these phrases. Put a check below your confidence level.

not confident	a little confident	somewhat confident	very confident

LEARN 1

A. Here are some phrases for encouraging self-correction. Listen and repeat. 6.4

Encouraging Self-Correction

What's missing?

There's a word missing.

What is wrong with this sentence?

Does this verb look right?

Try adding another word.

Try using another tense.

Please look at this sentence again.

Look at the difference between "like" and "likes.

This sentence is off topic.

Pay attention to the verbs.

Remember the irregular form.

Compare your work to the example.

Check spelling.

Please revise this sentence.

You need to pay attention to the model.

B. There are many substitutions for these phrases. Listen and repeat. 6.5

Phrases	Substitutions
There's a word missing.	There's a verb missing.
What is wrong with this sentence?	What is wrong with this word/answer/example/ question?
Does this verb look right?	Does this word sound right?
Try adding another word.	Try adding a verb.
Try using another tense.	Try using a different word.
Please look at this sentence again.	Please look at this list/chart/word/answer/example/ question again.
Look at the difference between "like" and "likes."	Compare "like" and "likes."
This sentence is off topic.	This paragraph is off topic.
Pay attention to the verbs.	Pay attention to the example/word order/ instructions. Pay attention to the information in the chart.
Remember the irregular form.	Don't forget the irregular form.
Compare your work to the example.	Compare your sentence to the example.
Check spelling.	Check the verbs/chart. Check word order.
Please revise this sentence.	Please review your verbs. Please rewrite this paragraph.
You need to pay attention to the model.	You need to review the example. You need to rewrite this sentence.

LEARN 2

Read the conversation, and watch the video. Listen to the teacher encourage self-correction. 6.3

Workbook example:

Pete is shorter John.

Pete is shorter than John.

Mrs. Sato: Look at the picture in the workbook. Who can compare Pete and John?

Takeshi: "John is tall than Pete."

Mrs. Sato: Does that sound right? What's missing?

Takeshi: Do I add *-er*?

Mrs. Sato: Yes. Remember to add *-er*.

Takeshi: "John is taller than Pete."

Mrs. Sato: Well done! OK, now work on your own. Write three sentences comparing Pete and John. Pay attention to the example... Yumi, please write a sentence on the board.

Yumi: OK.

Mrs. Sato: Please revise this sentence. Compare your work with the example.

Yumi: Is this OK?

Mrs. Sato: Yes, that's right! Excellent.

PRACTICE 1

Fill in the blanks with the phrases.

a different word	follow the example	off topic	sound right	verb look right
at this sentence again	difference between these two words	to the information in the chart	work to the example	wrong with this sentence

1. Does "like" ______________________________?
2. Remember to ______________________________.
3. Does this ______________________________?
4. Try using ______________________________.
5. Compare your ______________________________.
6. What is ______________________________?
7. Look at the ______________________________.
8. This sentence is ______________________________.
9. Pay attention ______________________________.
10. Please look ______________________________.

PRACTICE 2

Read the student's comparative sentences. Then fill in the blanks with the words or phrases to complete the corrections.

adding *-er*	off topic	rewrite this sentence	the verb	with this sentence
missing	revise	spelling	to add "than"	word order

1. *A pencil cheap than a pen.*
   Correction: Please ______________________ this sentence.
2. *Her house bigger is than my house.*
   Correction: Check ______________________.
3. *Math is than English.*
   Correction: What's ______________________?
4. *This street is longner than that street.*
   Correction: Check ______________________.
5. *English are easier than math.*
   Correction: Check ______________________.

6. *I jump high than you.*
   Correction: Try ______________________.

7. *I like to read.*
   Correction: This sentence is ______________________.

8. *A car is nicer a bicycle.*
   Correction: Don't forget ______________________.

9. *My book more I like than her book.*
   Correction: You need to ______________________.

10. *He is stronger than mine brother.*
    Correction: There is a problem ______________________.

PRACTICE 3

Read the answer key and the student's response. Then choose the correct feedback.

1. **ANSWER KEY:** The girl is taller than the boy.
   Student's Response
   The girl is tall than the boy.
   a. There is a verb missing.
   b. Remember to add *-er.*
   c. Try adding "more."

2. **ANSWER KEY:** He rode his bicycle to school.
   Student's Response
   He rode his bisicle to shcol.
   a. Check spelling.
   b. This sentence is off topic.
   c. What's missing?

3. **ANSWER KEY:** This book is more difficult than that book.
   Student's Response
   This book is difficult than that book.
   a. What's missing?
   b. Does the verb look right?
   c. Check spelling.

4. **ANSWER KEY:** She liked the game.
   Student's Response
   She likes the game.
   a. Try using another tense.
   b. There's a word missing.
   c. Pay attention to word order.

5. **ANSWER KEY:** Were you in class yesterday?
   Student's Response
   You were yesterday in class?
   a. Does "were" sound right?
   b. Pay attention to word order.
   c. Try using another tense.

6. **ANSWER KEY:** My sister has six cookies.
   Student's Response
   My sister has six cookie.
   a. The verb is wrong.
   b. What's wrong with this sentence?
   c. Try using another tense.

7. **ANSWER KEY:** Amanda brushes her hair every morning.
   Student's Response
   Amanda likes cats.
   a. This sentence is off topic.
   b. What's missing?
   c. Check word order.

8. **ANSWER KEY:** He will eat lunch now.
   Student's Response
   He will eats lunch now.
   a. What's missing?
   b. Does the verb look right?
   c. Pay attention to the instructions.

9. **ANSWER KEY:** He is playing basketball.
   Student's Response
   Playing he is basketball.
   a. Please review your verbs. Remember to add *-ing*.
   b. Compare your sentence to the example. This sentence is off topic.
   c. Check word order. Please rewrite this sentence.

10. **ANSWER KEY:** Some students did better than others on the test.
    Student's Response
    I played tennis.
    a. This sentence is off topic.
    b. Check the verbs. What's missing?
    c. Does "test" sound right? Try using a different word.

REFLECT

Think about what you learned in this lesson. Write five phrases you practiced.

Phrases for Encouraging Self-Correction

Now rate your confidence using these phrases. Put a check below your confidence level.

not confident	a little confident	somewhat confident	very confident

LESSON 4 REVIEW

1 Fill in the blanks with the words and phrases. Then practice saying the teacher's lines.

Don't forget to	Remember	right	That's not quite right.	Well done!

Teacher: Can someone give me an example of school rules? ________________, use "don't" in the rule.
Student: "Run don't in the hallway."... I mean, "Don't run in the hallway."

Teacher: ________________ You paid attention to word order. Next?
Student: "No talk in the hallway."

Teacher: ________________ follow the example.
Student: "Don't talk in the hallway."

Teacher: That's ________________. How about one more example?
Student: "Don't bringing toys to school."

Teacher: ________________ The verb is wrong.
Student: "Don't bring toys to school."

2 Read the answer key and the student's response. Then choose the correct feedback.

1. ANSWER KEY: I like reading, but it's difficult.
Student's Response
I like reading it's difficult.
a. Does "like" sound right?
b. What's missing?
c. The verb is wrong.

2. ANSWER KEY: We have ten apples.
Student's Response
We have the ten apples.
a. Try using another tense.
b. Don't forget to use *-ies*.
c. Don't add "the."

3. ANSWER KEY: She went to the birthday party.
Student's Response
She went to the birthday.
a. The sentence is incomplete.
b. Remember we're talking about the past.
c. There's a problem with this paragraph.

4. ANSWER KEY: The girl went to the beach.
Student's Response
The girl went to the beach.
a. Check your spelling.
b. Well done!
c. This word is wrong.

5. ANSWER KEY: I went to the game.
Student's Response
I will go to the game.
a. Try adding a word.
b. What's missing?
c. Try using another tense.

3 Read the chart and the student's response. Then fill in the blank with the word that completes the feedback.

1. **CHART**

   Present Continuous Examples

I	am	eating.
They	are	studying.

   Student's Response

   I am read.

   The verb is ________________.

2. **CHART**

   Plural Noun Examples

I	have	two dogs.
Tom	likes	many games.

   Student's Response

   I like many gams.

   ________________ your spelling.

3. **CHART**

   Comparative Examples

I	am	shorter	than you.
She	is	taller	than Tom.

   Student's Response

   Tom is shorter than Mary.

   Well ________________!

4. **CHART**

   Future Tense Examples

I	will leave	quickly.
He	will drive	safely.

   Student's Response

   John will drive safe.

   There's a ________________ with this sentence.

5. **CHART**

   Word Order Examples

   I have a yellow cat.

   The tree has a new, green leaf.

   Student's Response

   The girl has a blue, new sweater.

   Don't ________________ to follow the example.

UNIT 7 PUTTING IT TOGETHER

1. **Choose the two lesson goals that ask students to speak.**

   In this lesson, students will:
   a. read a paragraph about activities people do every day.
   b. listen to people describe their days.
   c. discuss what the people in the picture are doing.
   d. write about things they like and don't like to do every day.
   e. ask and answer questions about their daily routines.

2. **Read the activity instructions. Then read the statement and choose *True* or *False*.**

   Instructions: *Use the vocabulary to write sentences. Underline the verbs in the sentences.*

   The students need a pen or a pencil. True False

3. **Read the textbook activity. Then choose the correct question for the teacher.**

> My name is Li. I am from Taiwan. I am 17 years old. During the summer vacation I like to be with my friends. We all have jobs, but we see each other a few times during the week. Sometimes we go to the mall. Sometimes we see a movie. I work at an ice cream shop. I work three days a week. I like my job. Many families come in the shop. The children are always happy to get ice cream. One of my friends works there, too. We are a good team. She scoops the ice cream, and I take the money.

Teacher: __________
Student: One of her friends.
Teacher: That's right.

a. Who takes the money?
b. Who comes in the shop?
c. Who works with Li?
d. Who is happy to get ice cream?

4. **Read the audio script. Choose the sentence you can use to introduce this listening exercise.**

> **Audio Script:**
> Who is the king of the jungle? Many say that tigers are. Tigers are the largest wild cats in the world. Some adult tigers can weigh up to 363 kilograms. They are carnivores. They eat large mammals such as deer, wild pigs, antelope, and buffalo. Tigers are good swimmers. They like water, and they often swim in cool streams and ponds. They are also fast runners. They can run up to 65 kilometers per hour. Each tiger is unique. The stripes on every tiger are different, so no two tigers are the same. A tiger's roar can be heard three kilometers away, so you will know when a tiger is coming!

a. Today we are going to listen to a story about a tiger.
b. Now, we are going to listen to facts about tigers.
c. Next, we are going to listen to information about jungle animals.
d. Now, we are going to listen to an interview with a zookeeper.

5. **To greet your students, you say:**

a. It was good.
b. Fine, thank you.
c. Thank you.
d. How are you?

6. **Use the key words to write a phrase for taking attendance.**

Please/"here"/call/name ____

7. **To ask students about the weather, you say:**

a. Yesterday was windy.
b. How's the weather?
c. It's hot.
d. What day is today?

8. **You want the students to give you their homework now. You say:**

a. Please bring your homework tomorrow.
b. Please pass your homework to me.
c. Please take out your homework.
d. Please exchange papers with a partner.

9. **You want to make an announcement. You say:**

a. Please listen carefully.
b. Please copy from the board.
c. The test has 10 questions.
d. Please write it down.

10. You want to review the topic from the previous lesson. You say:

a. Here is your homework.
b. Tomorrow we will have a test.
c. What did we do yesterday?
d. Today we will talk about sports.

11. You want to change activities. You say:

a. Put your pencils down.
b. Please pay attention.
c. Let's move on to the next activity.
d. Turn over your paper.

12. Choose two sentences that communicate lesson goals.

a. What did we learn yesterday?
b. In this unit you are going to learn about the ocean.
c. Let's review what we learned today.
d. Today we are going to practice the new vocabulary.
e. Yesterday, we talked about these new words.

13. Choose the two lesson instructions that ask your students to read or write.

a. Talk to your partner.
b. Fill in the blanks.
c. In pairs, talk about your family.
d. Discuss the following questions.
e. Rewrite the paragraph in the past tense.

14. Look at the worksheet and the key words. Then write instructions for the worksheet using the key words.

___

Worksheet:	Key Words:
1. She played tennis yesterday. 2. The children went to the park last weekend.	Circle/past tense verb/each/sentence

15. Choose the sentence that engages students in the topic.

a. Talk with your partner.
b. Please pay attention.
c. Think about the family words you know.
d. Raise your hand.

16. You want students to say what you say. You say:

a. Read the first example please.
b. Here's an example.
c. Please listen to the example.
d. Please repeat after me.

17. Read the example from the textbook. Write a new example using the key words. Remember to capitalize and punctuate your sentence.

Example from Textbook:

Present Continuous

I am eating lunch.

She is sleeping.

We are swimming.

Key Words

He/play/soccer

____

____

18. Choose three sentences that encourage participation.

a. Who wants to volunteer?
b. Good job!
c. Do you want to try?
d. Please stand up.
e. Do you want to do number two, please?

19. Your students are shy. You want to motivate them. You say:

a. How are you?
b. We will learn new words today.
c. You can do it.
d. Work with a partner.

20. Read the language chart and task. Then read the student's response. Choose the correct response.

Language Chart:
Regular past tense: infinitive verb + *-ed*
Example: They watched a movie yesterday.

Task: Write a sentence about what you did yesterday.

Student's response: I walk to school yesterday.
You say:

a. Good job!
b. That's correct.
c. There is an extra word in the sentence.
d. That's not quite right.

21. You are reviewing the grammar lesson. Choose two correct statements.

You say:

a. Are there any questions about the vocabulary?
b. Are there any questions about the past tense?
c. We are going to begin the grammar lesson.
d. Let's look at the grammar again.
e. Who can tell me what we are going to do?

22. Choose the correct sentence to complete the missing lesson goal.

First, we are going to read.
Next, you will write sentences.

____

Finally, you are going to correct your partner's sentences.

a. Then, you will exchange papers with a partner.
b. Finally, you will turn in your papers.
c. Next, you will open your books.
d. First, we are going to listen to a story.

23. The class is completing a worksheet. Two students are talking. You say:

a. Please raise your hand.
b. Please get to work.
c. Please listen.
d. Please take turns.

24. A student uses his first language to ask you to say the instructions again. You say:

a. Please ask me again. I did not hear you.
b. Ask me in English. Say "Can you speak louder, please?"
c. Ask me again. Say "Can you speak slowly, please?"
d. Ask me in English. Say "Can you repeat that, please?"

25. You want a student to show something to the class. You say:

a. Clear your desk and push in your chair.
b. Line up and get ready for recess.
c. Stand up and come to the front.
d. Please go to your seat.

26. Choose the correct missing words.

____________________ away your pencils. Turn ____________________ your papers.

a. Put, over
b. Work, out
c. Pair, on
d. Take, under

27. You want students to work with a partner. Choose two correct instructions.

a. Pair up.
b. Please work by yourself.
c. Count off by twos.
d. Work in groups of three.
e. Work alone.

28. It's time for recess. You say:

a. Get ready for lunch.
b. Please go to your seats and sit down.
c. Push in your chairs and line up.
d. Turn over your papers.

29. Read the passage. Then read the teacher's question and the student's response. Is the student correct? Choose *Yes* or *No*.

> Saren Lay is from Cambodia. She came to the United States with her parents in 2002. She was 16 years old. She went to high school in Chicago. English was difficult for her at first. She worked hard in school and made new friends. They helped her learn to speak English well.
>
> After high school, she went to university to become a doctor. She also worked at a restaurant. She was very busy. She could not see her family or friends often.
>
> Now Saren is a doctor at a big hospital. She is married and has three children, two sons and one daughter.

Teacher: What is Saren's job now?
Student: She works at a restaurant.

Is the student correct?

a. Yes
b. No

30. Read the student's incorrect sentence. Choose the correct response.

Student: I go to the park yesterday.

You say:

a. I go to park.
b. I went to the park.
c. I goes to the park.
d. I go to the parks.

31. Read the homework assignment and grammar chart. Then choose the correct response to the student's work.

Homework Assignment: Rewrite the sentences with *be going to.*
Juan works in Mexico City.
We eat at an Italian restaurant.
The children play baseball.

Be going to				
I	***am***			
You	***are***	***going to***	**+**	**base form of the verb (*go, have, play, etc.*)**
She/He/It	***is***			

Student's Response: Juan be going to work in Mexico City.

a. Look at the grammar chart again.
b. That's correct.
c. Please check your spelling.
d. You have an extra word.

32. A student forgot his homework. You say:

a. Please take out your homework.
b. Anna will collect your homework.
c. Please put your papers on my desk.
d. Please bring your homework next time.

33. Students finished the test. Choose two correct instructions.

a. Please pass your tests to me.
b. I will read the instructions.
c. Put away your books.
d. Clear your desks.
e. Put your pencils down.

34. You want to know if students understand the conversation topic. You say:

a. I'll repeat the instructions.
b. Who is your partner?
c. Please raise your hand.
d. So, what are we going to talk about?

35. A student asks in their first language how to write a word. You say:

When you want to write a word, say: "____"

a. Please come to the board.
b. How do you spell that?
c. Can you speak more slowly?
d. What does it mean?

36. Read the situation. Then choose two correct responses.

The topic of the next unit is free-time activities. What are two ways you can get students to talk about this topic?

a. Tell students there will be a quiz on free-time activities.
b. Ask students to interview a partner about activities they do in their free time.
c. Ask students to talk about jobs.
d. Write a list of free-time activities on the board.
e. Show pictures of people doing different free-time activities. Tell students to think about what they see.

37. You write the word "fruit" on the board. You give one example, "apple." You want to ask students for another example. You say:

a. Can you think of a different fruit?
b. Is "apple" a fruit?
c. Let me give you another example.
d. What is an orange?

38. You want to summarize the day's lesson. You say:

a. Tomorrow we are going to practice verbs.
b. Let's review what we learned today.
c. Do you have your homework?
d. Look at the examples in your workbook.

39. Choose the correct missing words.

_______ homework, complete the exercise _______ page 7 _______ the workbook.

a. About, for, from
b. On, at, in
c. From, at, on
d. For, on, in

40. Write a sentence to dismiss the class. Use the key words. Remember to capitalize and punctuate your sentence.

____

Key Words:
Class/finished **good/afternoon**

CROSS REFERENCE CHART FOR RESEARCH BRIEFS

The Research Briefs that introduce Units 1-6 include references that apply to other lessons across the six units. This chart shows which lessons each research brief supports.

UNIT	RESEARCH BRIEF					
	1	2	3	4	5	6
1. Managing the Classroom: The learning environment						
Greeting students	•	•				
Discussing the date & weather	•					
Taking attendance	•					
Reviewing and collecting student work	•					
Making announcements	•					
Assigning homework	•					
Dismissing the class	•	•				
2. Managing the Classroom: Setting up learning opportunities						
Using classroom materials		•	•			
Teaching classroom language		•				
Directing students		•	•			
Giving test and quiz instructions		•		•		
Changing activities		•	•			
Disciplining		•				
Checking students understanding		•			•	
Encouraging participation	•	•				
Motivating students	•	•				•
3. Understanding Lesson Content: Planning content for student understanding						
Understanding instructions in student materials			•			
Understanding listening texts in student materials			•			
Understanding reading texts in student materials			•			
Writing content from student materials			•			
4. Communicating Lesson Content: Engaging students						
Understanding and communicating lesson goals				•		
Engaging students in the topic		•		•		
Explaining lesson content			•	•		
Modeling and giving examples		•		•		
Asking for and writing student examples				•		
Giving activity instructions		•	•	•		
Organizing students			•	•		
5. Assessing Student work: Using formative assessment to correct students						
Identifying and correcting written errors					•	•
Identifying and correcting spoken errors					•	•
Assessing student comprehension				•	•	•
6. Giving Feedback: Encouraging student independence						
Giving positive feedback		•				•
Encouraging self-correction					•	•

REFERENCES

Ames, C., & Ames, R. (1981). Competitive versus individualistic goal structures: The salience of past performance information for causal attributions and affect. *Journal of Educational Psychology*, *73*(3), 411–418.

Anderman, L., Andrzejewski, C., & Allen, J. (2011). How do teachers support students' motivation and learning in the classroom? *Teachers College Record*, *113*(5), 969–1003.

Archer, A., & Hughes, C. (2010). *Explicit instruction: Effective and efficient teaching*. New York: Guilford Press.

Baron, R. A. (1988). Negative effects of destructive criticism: impact on conflict, self-efficacy, and task performance. *Journal of Applied Psychology*, *73*(2), 199–207. https://doi.org/10.1037/0021-9010.73.2.199

Beesley, A. D., & Apthorp, H. (Eds.). (2010). *Classroom instruction that works: Research report* (2nd ed.). Denver, CO: McREL International.

Bitchener, J. (2008). Evidence in support of written corrective feedback. *Journal of Second Language Writing, 17*, 102–118.

Black, P., & Wiliam, D. (2009). Developing the theory of formative assessment. *Educational Assessment, Evaluation and Accountability*, *21*(1), 5–31.

Brosh, H. (1996). Perceived characteristics of the effective language teacher. *Foreign Language Annals*, *29*(2), 125–136.

Butler, D. L., & Winne, P. H. (1995). Feedback and self-regulated learning: A theoretical synthesis. *Review of Education Research*, *65*(3), 245–281.

Chan, J. C. Y., & Lam, S-F. (2010). Effects of different evaluative feedback on students' self-efficacy in learning. *Instructional Science*, *38*, 37–58.

Cheng, H., & Dörnyei, Z. (2007). The use of motivational strategies in language instruction: The case of EFL teaching in Taiwan. *International Journal of Innovation in Language Learning and Teaching*, *1*(1), 153–174.

Collier-Meek, M., Johnson, A., Sanetti, L., & Minami, T. (2019). Identifying critical components of classroom management implementation. *School Psychology Review*, *48*(4), 348–361.

Cook, C., Fiat, A., Larson, M., Daikos, C., Slemrod, T., Holland, E., . . . Renshaw, T. (2018). Positive greetings at the door: Evaluation of a low-cost, high-yield proactive classroom management strategy. *Journal of Positive Behavior Interventions*, *20*(3), 149–159.

Crooks, T. J. (1988). The impact of classroom evaluation practices on students. *Review of Educational Research*, *58*(4), 438–481.

Curby, T., Rimm-Kaufman, S., & Abry, T. (2013). Do emotional support and classroom organization earlier in the year set the stage for higher quality instruction? *Journal of School Psychology*, *51*, 557–569.

Davies, P., & Pearse, E. (2000). *Success in English teaching*. Oxford, UK: Oxford University Press.

Deci, E. L., Koestner, R., & Ryan, M. R. (1999). A meta-analytic review of experiments examining the effects of extrinsic rewards on intrinsic motivation. *Psychological Bulletin*, *125*, 627–668.

DeKeyser, R. (2018). Task repetition for language learning: A perspective from skill acquisition theory. In M. Bygate (Ed.), *Learning language through task repetition* (pp. 27–41). Amsterdam: John Benjamins Publishing Company.

Dweck, C. S., Davidson, W., Nelson, S., & Enna, B. (1978). Sex differences in learned helplessness: II. The contingencies of evaluative feedback in the classroom and III. An experimental analysis. *Developmental Psychology*, *14*(3), 268–276.

Ellis, R. (2002). Methodological options in grammar teaching materials. In E. Hinkel & S. Fotos (Eds.), *New perspectives on grammar teaching in second language classrooms* (pp. 155–179). Mahwah, NJ: Lawrence Erlbaum.

Ellis, R., Sheen, Y., Murakami, M., & Takashima, H. (2008). The effects of focused and unfocused written corrective feedback in an English as a foreign language context. *System*, *36*, 353–371.

Farrokhi, F., & Modarres, V. (2012). The effects of two pre-task activities on improvement of Iranian EFL learners' listening comprehension. *Theory and Practice in Language Studies*, *2*(1), 144–150.

Ferris, D. R. (1995). Student reactions to teacher response in multiple-draft composition classrooms. *TESOL Quarterly*, *29*(1), 33–53.

Fong, C. J., Patall, E. A., Vasquez, A. C., & Stautberg, S. (2019). A meta-analysis of negative feedback on intrinsic motivation. *Educational Psychology Review*, *31*, 121–162.

Frey, N., & Fisher, D. (2010). Identifying instructional moves during guided learning. *The Reading Teacher*, *64*(2), 84–95.

Frisby, B., & Martin, M. (2010). Instructor-student and student-student rapport in the classroom. *Communication Education*, *59*(2), 146–164.

Guilloteaux, M., & Dörnyei, Z. (2008). Motivating language learners: A classroom-oriented investigation of the effects of motivational strategies on student motivation. *TESOL Quarterly*, *42*(1), 55–77.

Hall, G. (2016). Method, methods and methodology: Historical trends and current debates. In G. Hall (Ed.), *The Routledge handbook of English language teaching* (pp. 209–223). London, UK: Taylor & Francis.

Hattie, J., & Timperley, H. (2007). The power of feedback. *Review of Education Research*, *77*(1), 81–112.

Joe, H., Hiver, P., & Al-Hoorie, A. (2017). Classroom social climate, self-determined motivation, willingness to communicate, and achievement: A study of structural relationships in instructed second language settings. *Learning and Individual Differences*, *53*, 133–144.

Khajavy, G., Ghonosolly, B., Fatemi, A., & Choi, C. (2016). Willingness to communicate in English: A microsystem model in the Iranian EFL classroom context. *TESOL Quarterly*, *50*(1), 154–180.

Korpershoek, H., Harms, T., de Boer, H., van Kuijk, M., & Doolard, M. (2016). A meta-analysis of the effects of classroom management strategies and classroom management programs on students' academic, behavioral, emotional, and motivational outcomes. *Review of Educational Research*, *86*(3), 643–680.

Kounin, J. (1970). *Discipline and group management in classrooms*. New York, NY: Holt, Rinehart & Winston.

Krashen, S. D. (1982). *Principles and practice in second language acquisition*. Oxford, UK: Pergamon Press Inc.

Kumaravadivelu, B. (2003). *Beyond methods: Macrostrategies for language teaching.* New Haven, CT: Yale University Press.

Kumaravadivelu, B. (2005). *Understanding language teaching: From method to postmethod*. Mahwah, NJ: Lawrence Erlbaum Associates.

Lee, E. J. (2013). Corrective feedback preferences and learner repair among advanced ESL students. *System*, *41*, 217–230.

Leinhardt, G., Wedman, C., & Hammond, K. M. (1987). Introduction and integration of classroom routines by expert teachers. *Curriculum Inquiry*, *17*(Summer, 2), 135–176.

Leki, I. (1991). The preferences of ESL students for error correction in college-level writing classes. *Foreign Language Annals*, *24*(3), 203–218.

Liu, X., & Qu, D. (2014). Exploring the multimodality of EFL textbooks for Chinese college students: A comparative study. *RELC Journal, 45*(2), 135–150.

Lyster, R., & Ranta, L. (1997). Corrective feedback and learner uptake: Negotiation of form in communicative classrooms. *SSLA*, *20*, 37–66.

Mackey, A., Kanganas, A. P., & Oliver, R. (2007). Task familiarity and interactional feedback in child ESL classrooms. *TESOL Quarterly, 41*(2), 285–312.

Marzano, R., & Pickering, D. (2003). *Classroom management that works: Research-based strategies for every teacher*. Alexandria, VA: Association for Supervision and Curriculum Development.

Nemati, M., Alavi, S. M., & Mohebbi, H. (2019). Assessing the effect of focused direct and focused indirect written corrective feedback on explicit and implicit knowledge of language learners. *Language Testing in Asia*, *9*(7), 1–18.

Nicol, D. J., & Macfarlane-Dick, D. (2006). Formative assessment and self-regulated learning: A model and seven principles of good feedback practice. *Studies in Higher Education*, *31*(2), 199–218.

Noels, K. A., Clément, R., & Pelletier, L. G. (1999). Perceptions of teachers' communicative style and students' intrinsic and extrinsic motivation. *The Modern Language Journal*, *83*(1), 23–34.

Pearson, D., & Gallagher, M. (1983). The instruction of reading comprehension. *Contemporary Educational Psychology*, *8*, 317–344.

Seidel, T., Rimmele, R., & Prenzel, M. (2005). Clarity and coherence of lesson goals as a scaffold for student learning. *Learning and Instruction*, *15*, 539–556.

Sheen, Y. (2010). Differential effects of oral and written corrective feedback in the ESL classroom. *Studies in Second Language Acquisition*, *32*, 203–234.

Sonbul, S., & Schmitt, N. (2009). Direct teaching of vocabulary after reading: Is it worth the effort? *ELT Journal*. *64*(3), 253–260.

Swain, M. (1993). The output hypothesis: Just speaking and writing aren't enough. *The Canadian Modern Language Review*, *50*, 158–164.

Swain, M. (2005). The output hypothesis: Theory and research. In E. Hinkel (Ed.), *Handbook of research in second language teaching and learning* (pp. 471–483). Mahwah, NJ: Lawrence Erlbaum Associates.

Tomlinson, B. (2011). Introduction. In B. Tomlinson (Ed.), *Materials development in language teaching*. Cambridge, UK: Cambridge University Press.

Tsang, W. K. (2004). Feedback and uptake in teacher-student interaction: An analysis of 18 English lessons in Hong Kong secondary classrooms. *Regional Language Centre Journal*, *35*(2), 187–209.

Vold, E. T. (2020). Meaningful and contextualized grammar instruction: What can foreign language textbooks offer? *The Language Learning Journal, 48*(2), 133–147.

Walsh, S., & Li, L. (2013). Conversations as space for learning. *International Journal of Applied Linguistics*, *23*(2), 247–266.

NOTES:

NOTES:

NOTES:

NOTES:

NOTES:

NOTES:

NOTES:

NOTES:

NOTES:

NOTES:

NOTES:

NOTES:

NOTES: